how to mend your treasured porcelain, china, glass, and pottery

how to mend your treasured porcelain, china, glass, and pottery

LAURENCE ADAMS MALONE

RESTON PUBLISHING COMPANY, INC.
Reston, Virginia
A Prentice-Hall Company

Library of Congress Cataloging in Publication Data

Malone, Laurence Adams.
  How to mend your treasured porcelain, china, glass, &
pottery.

  Includes index.
  1. Pottery—Repairing. 2. Glassware—Repairing.
1. Title.
NK4233.M29   738.1   75–29151
ISBN 0–87909–344–7

10 9 8 7 6 5 4 3 2 1

Printed in the United States of America.

contents

v

preface

I would like to express my appreciation to Charles N. Heckelman and Nettie Allen Voges for their assistance in the reorganization of this manuscript. Mrs. Voges undertook a great deal of research into the vast field of the art of making china, glass, and pottery. Her task lay in reducing volumes of background information to a few highly definitive paragraphs applicable to mending, repairing, and restoring.

My special thanks must also be extended to Patricia Dalzell who through her skill as a photographer has shown step-by-step instructions, adding to the lesson value of this book. And also I am very grateful to Philip and Vera Muller, owners of the Boehm bird pictured in Chapter 3.

The professional views and assertions regarding the mending materials and their application as systems for mending, repairing, and restoring china, glass, and pottery are the author's and are not to be construed as those of others practicing the art as a profession.

LAURENCE ADAMS MALONE

chapter one

---

you can do it!

Articles made of china, glass, and pottery are generally fragile and may be easily cracked, chipped, or broken. Among the many articles made of these materials are such rare and costly pieces as porcelain produced and decorated in the Meissen factories of Germany, the lifelike birds of Boehm, and crystal produced by Waterford, Baccarat, and Steuben. There are also less valuable articles either inherited or collected that are treasured for a variety of personal reasons. And there are the practical and useful articles to be found in every household: Table services of all three materials and articles that come in pairs and sets such as glasses, vases, and pitchers. Some of these may not be costly, but they may be difficult to replace.

Whenever a good article has been damaged, the first reaction of the owner may be, "Oh, if this hadn't happened!" The second is apt to be, "Can it be mended?"

The answer is "Yes." It *can* be restored, not glued together to be shelved in a protected place, but really *made whole again.*

Setting up a home work area with a workbench and a few items of equipment.

3

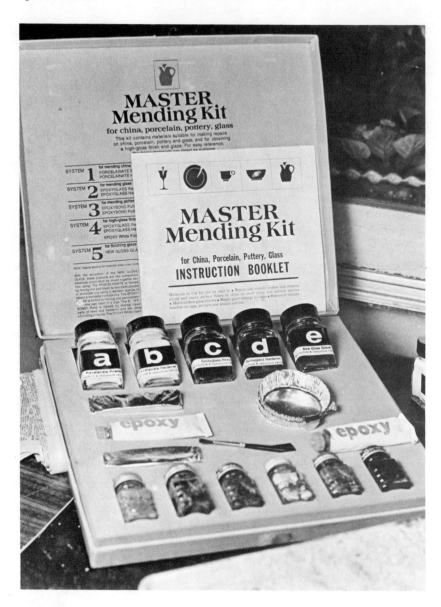

*The Master
Mending Kit.*

Cracks and chips can be invisibilized. Missing pieces that have been lost—even missing handles from cups and pitchers—can be satisfactorily replaced. A cup with a mended or restored handle can be trusted to contain hot beverages without risk of accident. Best of all, *you can do it!* With the materials recommended in this book, a novice can achieve satisfying, professional-looking results from the beginning, *provided*—and this is worth stating twice—*provided that:*

1.   Mending the broken article is worth the time and effort required to do a good job.

If the piece under consideration is old, one of a pair, or part of a set, the owner might profitably check its value or replacement cost in comparison with the *time* required to do a satisfactory job and the relatively small *cost* of mending materials. Many table service articles, purchased easily from open stock, may no longer be available except by special order at premium prices.

2.   The best mending materials are used for each job.

The author has designed a Master Mending Kit* that contains the mending materials he prefers to use, in sufficient quantities to do a number of repair jobs. Refills or individual systems of these materials are readily available in larger quantities in most art supply and hardware stores as the skill and enthusiasm of the mender prompts the undertaking of larger and more elaborate mending projects.

Learning to mend broken articles of china, glass, and pottery is useful and practical. It can become a rewarding and profitable hobby. And a mending kit is as essential in a well-organized household as a first-aid kit, a sewing box, or a tool chest.

3.   A small but adequate work area is set up.

This is important, because articles that are in the process of being restored must be kept in a protected place while mending materials harden and decorations and glazes dry thoroughly.

4.   The step-by-step procedures for mending each type of material and each article, as outlined in this book, are carefully followed.

One step leads to the next in such a way that the mender, beginning the first job, need not be concerned about understand-

---

*The Master Mending Kit is produced by Atlas Minerals and Chemical Division of ESB, Inc., Mertztown, Pa.

ing the instructions for, say Step 9, until Step 8 has been completed.

5. A supply of simple equipment is collected in a box, basket, or other convenient container so that it may be at hand as needed.

A list of equipment such as scissors, masking tape, razor blades, sandpaper, and the like is given on pages 7–10. The importance of collecting equipment before beginning a mending job is that mending materials, once mixed, harden very quickly. There isn't time to hunt for a brush or a clothespin.

now to begin

The first step is to become familiar with the mending materials that are to be used. These are *epoxys*—that is, bonding resins, characterized by toughness, strong adhesion, and high corrosion resistance. They are different from glue, which is generally the product of boiling together the bones, cartilage, and connective tissue of animals. Epoxy produces an adhesive. Broken articles that are epoxybonded become whole again. Articles mended with epoxybond resin will not come apart, even in the dishwasher. Those that have been put together with glue may come apart when placed in hot water, exposed to dampness, or during ordinary usage.

what's in a good mending kit?

The following list refers to materials suitable for making repairs and obtaining a high-gloss finish and glaze. These are grouped and listed as Systems:

System 1   *For mending china*

Porcelainate Powder
Porcelainate Hardener (liquid)

Two parts of powder are mixed with one part of liquid. The mixture should be used within 18 minutes.

System 2   *For mending glass*

Epoxyglass Resin (liquid)
Epoxyglass Hardener (liquid)

> Equal parts of each are mixed. This mixture should be used within 15 minutes. When mixing, add the Epoxyglass Resin to the Epoxyglass Hardener. This reduces the possibility of bubbles appearing in the mixture.

System 3   *For mending pottery*

Epoxybond Putty Resin (solid)
Epoxybond Putty Hardener (solid)

> Equal parts of each are mixed. This mixture should be used within 30 minutes.

System 4   *For high gloss finishing (porcelainizing)*

Epoxyglass Resin (liquid)
Epoxyglass Hardener (liquid)
Epoxybond Resin (white finishing paste)

> Equal parts of the liquids are mixed. The paste is added as needed. The mixture should be used within 15 minutes.

System 5   *For glazing and finishing* (liquid)

> This may be used directly from the bottle with a brush as needed.

> A complete mending kit should also contain the six basic colors needed for tinting and decorating. White Epoxybond Paste can be used with the colors. Other necessary materials are brushes, spatulas, and containers for mixing.

equipment

> This is a list of equipment recommended for use in all step-by-step sequences given for mending specific articles of china (Chapter 3), glass (Chapter 4), and pottery (Chapter 5).

brushes   Three or four, of varying size and thickness. Acrylic bristle brushes with unpainted wooden handles are preferred.

razor blades   Single edge, for trimming away excess materials.

small spatulas   For use in making various kinds of cement mixes. A box of assorted wooden tongue depressors is useful for this purpose.

small saucer   Of china or glass (never plastic!), for use in mixing various materials. A small, flat white porcelain tray is useful for mixing various kinds of stiff clay epoxy material. A slightly smaller curved saucer (about 3 inches in diameter) is excellent for runny- or syrupy-type cements that go through a thickening stage before becoming a workable paste.

wipers   Either paper napkins or paper towels, in handy packets. Cheesecloth cut in convenient small squares is also useful for this purpose.

apron   A heavy denim workman's apron is excellent—it contains pockets for pencils and for wet and dry cloths. The apron should be large enough to protect clothing.

good light   For small mending jobs that can be done quickly, good window light or a 100-watt bulb is recommended, particularly for use in damp and humid weather when the heat from the bulb aids in drying the cementing materials. A gooseneck stand is recommended, because it can be easily adjusted.

sandbox   Any sturdy box large enough to hold articles that are being mended can be partly filled (to a depth of 3 to 4 inches) with coarse, white sand. Suitable, clean sand is generally available in pet shops. Articles that are being mended can be propped in the sandbox while work is in progress and during the hardening period. If an article is heavy, tongue depressors can support it in the sandbox.

snap-on type wooden clothespins   These are used for clamping together two or more pieces of material until masking tape can be properly applied. They also serve to hold pieces in place, giving perfect evenness in matching the pieces, while quick adjustments are made. Metal hand clamps are also useful, particularly for holding together large pieces.

masking tape   Rolls of several widths should be at hand. Masking tape is used to secure one piece to another as cement material hardens, and to hold pieces in place as additional pieces are added. It also serves to protect mended joints from sand. Masking tape is used in mending like adhesive tape is used in bandaging, and pre-torn strips in various lengths are kept conveniently at hand as work progresses.

metal waste basket   For catching all debris quickly.

heavy-gauge type aluminum wire	To serve as the structural core when building handles on cups, bowls, pots, pitchers, and other articles requiring strong handles. Any alternate procedures are included in the step-by-step sequences.
enamel pan or bucket	Large enough to hold articles that have been previously mended and that need to be cleaned by boiling.
sandpaper	In assorted sizes and finest grinds, cut in 4-inch squares.
soft wax	For making molds. A form of plastic impression material, also useful for this purpose, is available from dental supply houses.
nails	Several sizes.
heavy bread board	Or similar board in which nails can be driven, to aid in holding some types of articles that are being mended.
marking pencils and tracing paper (onion skin)	For use in copying designs to restore a mended article to its original appearance.
scotch tape	Rolls of several widths should be on-hand. This serves the same general purpose as masking tape, but is used more frequently in mending articles of glass.
scissors and tweezers	Several sizes of both are useful and should be kept with the mending equipment.
rubber bands	A box of assorted sizes will be helpful. After mending material has been applied and the pieces held firmly by a clothespin or two, rubber bands can be added (around a cup or similar article) to hold the broken pieces firmly while the cement hardens.
mortite **or**	This is a commercial putty-like material, ordinarily used for caulking and stripping purposes. It comes in round strips wound around a cardboard form, and is easily handled.
plasticine	Plasticine serves to help hold together two or three pieces in a mend, and is particularly useful when putting together very small pieces that are too little for clamps, rubber bands, or for standing in the sandbox. It is available in most toy shops.
small glass pots	For holding water and thinner.
nutpick	Or similar metal instrument for use in getting into cracks and other small areas.
handgrinder	This is a small electrical appliance that is found in many home workshops where it is used to sand and refinish all kinds of sur-

faces—plaster patches, woodwork, table tops, and others. It is also useful in mending china, glass, and pottery. The handgrinder comes with an assortment of hard and soft rubber wheels, drills, stone-grinding discs, and a carborundum cutting disc. If a new handgrinder is to be purchased, one that is housed in a bakelite case rather than in a plastic case is recommended.

Suggestions for learning to use a handgrinder in mending   General directions for use of this appliance are given in the manual that comes with it, and this should be studied carefully. When a handgrinder is used in mending china, glass, and pottery, these suggestions will be helpful.

Experiment on any piece of useless broken china or pottery. Try making an "X," a "V," and a tic-tac-toe grid. Practice cutting a "V" groove in a cracked edge and cutting a grid over a flake chip. Then, combine both for a cracked, flaked edge. Another good exercise is making a double "X" ("XX") or a butterfly in the edge of an old dish that is ready to be discarded.

cautionary information about mending materials

The products necessary for mending are sophisticated chemical compounds and should be used with caution. Keep all materials out of the reach of children. Before using such materials, please take a minute to read the following information:

Epoxyglass Resin, Epoxybond Putty Resin (System 3), and *Epoxy White Finishing Resin* contain epoxy resins that may cause an allergic skin reaction. Provide adequate ventilation, and avoid prolonged breathing of vapors. Wash hands with soap and water after using. In case of contact with eyes, flush with plenty of water, and call a physician.

New Gloss Glaze Coating contains volatile and toxic solvents. Keep away from heat, sparks, and open flame. Use with adequate ventilation. Avoid prolonged breathing of vapors or repeated contact with skin. Keep container tightly closed when not in use. In case of contact with skin, wash thoroughly with soap and water. If swallowed, do *not* induce vomiting; call a physician.

Porcelainate Powder contains alkaline silicate, which is harmful if swallowed and may cause eye irritation. In case of contact with eyes, flush with plenty of water, and call a physician. If swallowed, drink plenty of water, and call a physician.

Epoxybond Putty Resin and *Epoxybond Putty Hardener* (System 3) contain amine resins that may cause an allergic skin reaction. Provide adequate ventilation and avoid prolonged breathing of vapors. Wash hands with soap and water after using. In case of contact with eyes, flush with plenty of water, and call a physician.

Note: All repaired articles should be washed with soap and water, and allowed to dry prior to use. Porcelainate Hardener will freeze. Store at room temperature. If frozen, store at room temperature for 24 hours, and stir thoroughly before using.

There are three words that will be used frequently throughout this book, each referring to a way in which mending materials are used. These are *mend, repair,* and *restore.*
With the proper System, the materials are used:

> To *mend* a break
> To *repair* a damage
> To *restore* a missing part

If you understand the way in which each term is used, following the step-by-step sequences will be easier.

chapter two

---

miracle-mending
materials

how to use your materials

A mending-materials kit includes all the materials you need for mending chinaware, table service pieces, decorative accessories, fine porcelains, stoneware, and pottery. There are five systems of these materials and each has a mending use.

For any broken article: First, collect all the broken pieces, and assemble them so as not to mutilate any of their edges. They may not quite re-fit.

Study the problem: How would you fit them together? What is involved? You must examine their hardness and thickness to determine what kind of material with which to mend. In a few minutes of study, you will know what is involved in the mending problem.

the problems in mending

The problems in mending a broken piece are resolved by your decision about what steps to take, as well as what materials to use. You may have to consider the seriousness of the break. The scope of the work may be costly and time-consuming. It is true that you will have to count pieces as you count days. If you have 12 broken pieces, it will probably take you about 12 days to see them all properly cemented together. You will use System 1, 2, or 3, comprised of a self-hardening epoxy and resin chemical cement. You will have to apply it with a fairly stiff art brush to the edges of the largest piece and to the one to be joined to it. The kind of system you use will depend on your observation and analysis of what the piece is made of.

15

your approach

The piece you are mending will of itself alert you to some of the techniques you will need to develop. First, you may find that the first two pieces you cement are going to have to be clamped together and balanced in a sandbox until thoroughly dry before the next pieces can be joined to them. The size, thickness, and kind will determine for you how to approach the problem of what piece you are mending. If cementing or repairing a broken out piece, be sure all edges to be cemented are absolutely clean and free of any old glue or other mending material.

porcelain

If the broken pieces are made of "true" porcelain you will use System 1, Porcelainate Powder and Hardener. Porcelain is of two kinds. One kind is referred to as Hard Paste and is a true porcelain. The other kind is referred to as Soft Paste and is a semi-porcelain. A third kind of porcelain is known as bone china. Bone china is a compromise between hard paste and soft paste porcelain. All three are translucent, have a shell-like quality and appearance, and give a bell-like sound when struck. Bone china contains felspar, a silicate used in making glass. If the broken item is bone china, you would use System 2, as though you were mending glass. You may also combine System 2, the Epoxyglass Resin and Hardener, with System 4, the Epoxybond Resin White Finishing paste, to obtain a translucent porcelainized finish. When porcelain is made, it has to be fired. With these mending systems, no firing is necessary.

Making porcelain (china) requires high-temperature firing, because porcelain contains kaolin, which makes the finest of all ceramic artware. It is a hard vitreous body of clay that fires to a translucent, jewel-like white, sparkling, lustrous, and beautiful. Antique figurines and dinnerware made of porcelain (ball clay) are highly prized by collectors throughout the world. Any objects made of true porcelain are indeed worth repairing with painstaking care. You will not, however, be working as a ceramist does, with basic natural clay, but with mending materials such as Porcelainate Powder and Hardener, with non-firing epoxies and resins made to produce good mending results and to simulate the lustrous porcelain-like finish the article had before being damaged.

Stoneware, an earthenware or pottery, is different from porcelain. It is a hard, glassy, vitreous body, frequently called ironstone. The two words glassy and vitreous together call attention to the nature of its vitreous-type texture. Some kinds of stoneware are best mended with the same materials used to mend glassware—they are that glassy. If the texture glitters like granite, the name graniteware is often given to an article. When pieces of stoneware are fired, they first turn to varying shades of grey or brown. A mixture of firebrick clay produces the rough texture from which stoneware gets its name. Stoneware and pottery are similar. Pottery, which may also be called earthenware, is made of coarse clay hardened by heat. It is merely a firm but pliable kind of earth, not containing kaolin, which can be easily molded, shaped, fired, and hardened for commercial use. However, it may be well for you to note right here that pottery, like porcelain, has varieties of hardness and softness. Stoneware is a variety of hard pottery and you would in most instances use System 2 in mending it. To restore missing pieces you would probably use System 1, if the article more nearly resembles porcelain in appearance. System 3 may be used to advantage when the article more closely resembles the natural clays of the earth. System 3, Epoxybond Putty Resin and Hardener, looks like and hardens to the consistency of stone and should be used for mending hard vitreous pieces of ironstone or stoneware that have an earthenware-like quality. How you use your materials and the systems to which they apply is of paramount importance. And to do that expertly, you first should know whether the piece to be mended is hard paste porcelain or soft paste porcelain, hard paste pottery or soft paste pottery. It may be helpful for you to remember that some soft paste pottery is referred to as faience, or majolica. Almost everyone has some of these pieces as tableware, dinner, luncheon, and tea service, or as decorative accessories. The size and thickness, the decorative quality of the piece, all of these characteristics plus other identifying marks on the bottom of the item under the glaze are going to alert you to what is needed in the way of a mending system to restore, mend, or repair it.

right approach

In making the right approach to mending or restoring, you will have to fully realize what kind of an item you are working with. I cannot stress enough the importance of knowing what the item is made of. What is its basic substance? Porcelain, porcelain-like (glassy) bone china, stoneware (hard, vitreous) ironstone-type pottery or semi-hard porcelain (soft paste)? In every instance— mending, restoring, or repairing—it will pay off to realize what you are working with. It may be best, even with the small, thin-edged pieces, to use Porcelainate Powder and Hardener if there is follow-on painting and decorating to be done. The powder, when mixed as a paste and used to cement your pieces, whether large or small, can and must be sanded down until "the finger-nail test" reveals no detectable difference between the edges you have joined. The sanding itself prepares a surface which is suitable for paint. You will learn how easy it is to "feather" or spread out any covering edges to achieve a perfect match; this will cover any unsightly crack showing where you have joined the broken edges. This is only a hint. Exactly how to do it is explained in the step-by-step procedures.

The miracle-mending materials, all of them, are non-firing. Each comprise a system which may be used for large or small pieces and will set overnight to iron-like hardness. In making a decision about which of these materials to use, you may also want to know and remember that you can pre-color. I would recommend doing so on first try. As you become more skillful at mending, try these new techniques, which are rooted in the old, and in so doing, you may achieve some exciting results.

Last but not least, in your approach to the piece to be mended, if your article is stoneware and vitreous—that is, hard and glassy or almost granite-like in its basic composition—you will find it best to use Epoxyglass Resin and Hardener. System 2, when mixed in equal parts, sets up chemically in a self-heating, self-curing, rapid-drying process. This same epoxy and hardener, please note, will be what you will use to mend clear glass. The more glass-like and vitreous your china, the more inclined you will be to use this chemical mixture, and quite right you are. As you become familiar with these materials systems and make decisions as to which one to use, the mending procedure will become vastly easier, more exciting, and loads more fun.

system 1   for mending
china and stoneware

The first of the "miracle-mending materials" to learn about is called *Porcelainate.** It is a two-part system (System 1) and consists of a white powder and a white liquid hardener. These are complex compounds of the modern chemical laboratory. The Porcelainate powder is composed of zinc oxide and potassium

*Porcelainate was invented, patented, and so named by the author.

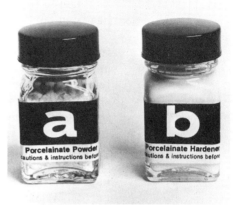

System 1 for mending chinaware and stoneware and for molding missing parts includes Porcelainate Powder and Porcelainate Hardener (available at most art supply and hardware stores).

silicate, both of which are highly adhesive and form an unbreakable bond. The white liquid hardener is a resinous substance. When properly combined, the powder and liquid form a putty-like material that can be easily molded with the fingers and which possesses the dynamics for mending all types of chinaware. This material is externally identical or interchangeable with porcelain and similar ceramics. In the putty-like stage, it can be formed into any shape, and it hardens *without firing*. It also exhibits a small degree of expansion, matching that of porcelain.

The length of time required for this two-part mixture to harden or set up, commonly referred to as the "pot life," is eighteen minutes. During this time, Porcelainate resembles white putty. It can be kneaded like dough with the fingers, is flexible, and is malleable. It is also non-corrosive. Although the pot life of the mixture is limited, the mender is not under pressure to work quickly against time. The pot life can be considerably extended if, in handling the mixture in the putty-like state, the fingers are dampened frequently in water; small quantities can be mixed as often as they are needed.

Porcelainate, in this putty-state, seems almost to gravitate of its own inclination toward the damages to china where missing sections and missing parts are needed. It can be shaped with the fingers into rim-breaks, pushed into cracks, and squeezed into flake-damaged areas. It can also be molded into new spouts and handles lost from a pitcher, cup, or similar article, and can be molded into finials and as missing ornamental parts of figurines. The material lends itself with remarkable versatility to the creativity and innovation of the mender. Then, by its own inherent alchemy, this soft, pliable, putty-like material which is so amenable to being handled, becomes stone-hard, and can be matched to the integral part of any article of china with which it has been bonded. Herein lies the miracle!

Because the pot life of Porcelainate rarely needs to exceed forty-five minutes, only a sufficient quantity of the white powder and white liquid hardener mixture should be prepared at one time to repair a specific area of damage. Leftover material cannot be stored for later use and, once it has hardened, can never again be softened. So the mender learns quickly to clean bits and scraps from spatulas, mixing dishes, and other equipment. Fingers are scrubbed, too. Remember that all chemical compounds should be used with caution and according to instructions, and should be kept out of the reach of children.

When Porcelainate is to be used in mending chinaware that has a background tint or shade or color, this can be and should be added to the two-part system as it is being mixed and kneaded. When using the paints provided in the Master Mending Kit or good quality oil paints (such as Grumbacher's) under good light, the mender is challenged to experiment until a satisfactory match is achieved. If the article being mended has a border design, a gold edge, or even an elaborate pattern of flowers, fruits, birds, or other decorative features, these can be added, but *after* the Porcelainate has had adequate time (at least 24 hours) to harden and to be bonded permanently to the china or stoneware. Suggestions and directions for decorating and for the use of gold materials—whether on a saucer or plate from a modern open-stock china or stoneware table service or a rare piece of antique Spode, Royal Crown Derby, or Meissen—are given in Chapter 6.

system 2 for mending glass

The second of the miracle-mending materials to learn about is also a two-part system (System 2). It is composed of two water-clear liquids, *Epoxyglass Resin* and *Epoxyglass Hardener*. When these two are mixed in equal parts in a small cup or dish, using a wooden spatula, they become a heavy, water-clear substance. The pot life of this mixture is fifteen minutes, so, again, only a small quantity is prepared at one time; however, with this mixture, as with Porcelainate, mending is not a race against time. One of the many admirable features of these two-part systems is that each part can wait patiently and inertly in bottle, tube, or wrapper, to be mixed in sufficient quantities to match both the pace and the requirements of the mender.

System 2 for mending glass, plastic, or jewelry in-
cludes Epoxyglass Resin and Epoxyglass Hardener
(available at most art supply and hardware stores).

Experience reveals that if you spoon out the Hardener first, and then ladle the Epoxyglass Resin into it, fewer bubbles, if any, occur. I cannot tell you why this is so, although, I suspect the Epoxyglass Resin is chemically the lighter-bodied of the two and mixes into the Hardener with less strength or agitation needed to blend it in. Notice, I did not say lighter weight. All I can tell you is it works better in reverse order, prohibiting bubbles when clear Epoxy materials are mixed for crystal.

If you forget to do this, and bubbles do form in the mix, pass the saucer in which you have made the mix over a gas flame until the dish is warm to the fingers. The bubbles will disappear; however, heating speeds up the setting process, so you must work much faster with your mending material. When a fresh mix is needed, try doing it right!

The Epoxyglass Resin and Epoxyglass Hardener mixture is *not* soluble in water; however, in working with it, brushes and fingers should be dipped frequently into solvent such as alcohol, acetone, or lacquer thinner made from petroleum distillates having a methylate base. Commercial products labeled "brush cleaner" will not remove this mixture from brushes and may even ruin them. When a thinner is used with the Resin and Hardener mix, the mender is able to achieve a smooth mend and give a finished appearance to the article being repaired.

As this mixture thickens, it can be applied with a brush to put together two or more pieces of a broken glass article. It can also be used to fill areas where pieces have been broken out and lost, provided that the areas are small—no larger than a quarter. The smaller the hole or broken-out area, the more nearly perfect the result. The mixture can be pushed into crevices and cracks and can be built up, one layer at a time, allowing for drying time between layers, until an area has been filled. This Epoxyglass mix will harden into a glass-like substance and, once married to an article, must be polished smooth and glazed without damage. Clean your brush immediately after use! The newly added material *looks like glass* and *feels like glass* but it is not glass. It is a bonding resin that is subject to slight ambering after the passing of time (noticeable after a year or more). The ambering effect can be delayed provided the mended article is not exposed to direct sunlight, and provided the mixture is very carefully tinted with blue (for crystalline clarity) or the appropriate color for colored clear glass.

When the Resin mix is used to mend glass articles that are not crystal clear—such as milk glass—use System 2. Colors may be added, according to directions for each type of tinted or colored glass, and the possibility of ambering is eliminated.

system 3
for mending pottery

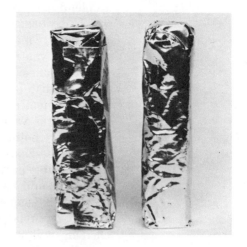

System 3 for mending stoneware and pottery and for making handles and other weight-bearing missing parts includes Epoxybond Putty Resin and Epoxybond Putty Hardener (available at most art supply and hardware stores).

The third of the miracle-mending materials to learn about is also a two-part system (System 3). It is composed of solid materials, *Epoxybond Putty Resin* and *Epoxybond Putty Hardener*.

These two materials, which are used for mending pottery, are prepared by working together with the fingers in a kneading, rolling motion until a complete blending has been achieved. If a tint or color is needed, this can be worked in, a little at a time, until a match with the article to be mended has been achieved.

The pot life of the putty mixture is considerably longer than that of Systems 1 and 2—about thirty minutes—and throughout the working period, the fingers can and should be used freely, dampening them with water from a small saucer or dish, and smoothing the putty into the areas where it is needed. It can be handled easily to fill cracks, nicks, and small broken out areas. It is also serviceable for making large pieces as well as new handles, spouts, finials, or whatever else may be required to repair even a very badly damaged pottery article.

Step-by-step procedures for use of this material are given in Chapter 5. Decorating types of pottery such as that found in gift shops, department stores, and antique shops is given in Chapter 6.

system 4   for porcelainizing (high gloss finishing)

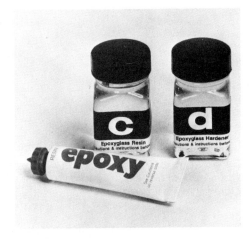

System 4 for porcelainizing (invisible china mending) includes Epoxyglass Resin, Epoxyglass Hardener, and Epoxybond Resin (White Finishing Paste) (available at most art supply and hardware stores).

The fourth of the miracle-mending materials to learn about is composed of two compounds previously introduced in System 2, *Epoxyglass Resin* and *Epoxyglass Hardener*, both water-clear liquids, with the addition of a third material, Epoxybond Resin, called *white finishing paste*. This is identfied as System 4.

The two liquids are mixed in equal parts, and the white finishing paste is worked in as it is needed. Color may be added to this three-part mixture to match the background shade or tint of the article that is being mended.

The pot life of this mixture is fifteen minutes; however,

as the material is being used, the brush may be moistened as often as necessary in solvent or lacquer thinner, as recommended for use in System 2. In this way, working time for use of the mixture can be extended, and additional mixes may be made as they are needed.

The porcelainizing finish is used *over* both Porcelainate (System 1) and Epoxybond Putty Resin (System 3)—that is, on articles of both china and pottery that have been satisfactorily mended, after adequate time has been allowed for hardening, at least 24 hours or more. Any decorating that is needed is added after the porcelainizing finish itself has completely hardened. The exception to this rule is the use of gold leafing, which is described in Chapter 6.

system 5   for finishing

System 5 for finishing and glazing after repairs includes New Gloss Glaze (available at most art supply and hardware stores).

The last of the miracle-mending materials to learn about is a water-clear glazing compound called *New Gloss Glaze* (System 5).* It may be applied directly from the bottle with a brush to any mended article of china, glass, pottery, or stoneware. If decorating is needed on an article that has been mended, New Gloss Glaze is used over the decorations with one exception, and this is important to remember. Gold materials must always be added *last*.

*New Gloss Glaze was invented, patented, and so named by the author.

additional materials needed to mend china, glass, and pottery

paints	Six colors are provided in the Master Mending Kit. These are: Red, brown, blue, yellow, green, and black. The following colors in oil paints (Grumbacher's) are also recommended: white, red, blue, yellow, umbers, siennas, Venetian red, and black.
solvent or lacquer thinner	Acetone or lacquer thinner made from petroleum distillates having a methylate base. Do not use commercial products labeled "brush cleaner."
gold pastes	For art gold finishes.
bronzing liquid	For bronze finishes.
wax (paraffin or candle wax)	For use in mending marble.
industrial peroxide or washing soda	For boiling and bleaching.
clorox	For bleaching by soaking.
water	

All of these materials should be collected and conveniently arranged in the mending area before work begins.

summary of systems (self-curing—no heat needed)

	MIX RATIO	POT LIFE*
SYSTEM 1 FOR MENDING PORCELAIN (CHINA)		
Porcelainate Powder	*2 parts to*	*18 minutes*
Porcelainate Hardener (Liquid)	*1 part*	
SYSTEM 2 FOR MENDING GLASS		
Epoxyglass Resin (Liquid)	*1 part to*	*15 minutes*
Epoxyglass Hardener (Liquid)	*1 part*	

*Pot life means the time in minutes between the mixing and hardening of these materials.

SYSTEM 3 FOR MENDING POTTERY	MIX RATIO	POT LIFE
Epoxybond Putty Resin (Solid)	*1 part to*	*30 minutes*
Epoxybond Putty Hardener (Solid)	*1 part*	

SYSTEM 4 FOR HIGH GLOSS FINISHING (*Porcelainizing*)

Epoxyglass Resin (Liquid)	*1 part to*	*15 minutes*
Epoxyglass Hardener (Liquid)	*1 part*	
Epoxybond Resin (White Finishing Paste, add as needed)		

SYSTEM 5 FOR FINISHING GLAZE

New Gloss Glaze (Liquid)	*1 part product (unlimited use, use as needed)*	

With the exception of the *New Gloss Glaze*, these products are two-component materials which must be mixed together before using. The Porcelainate powder, System 1, is mixed by adding one part liquid to two parts powder in a saucer using a wooden spatula to obtain a workable consistency. The Epoxyglass, System 2, is mixed by adding one part Resin to one part Hardener. This may also be combined by spooning the components into a saucer and mixing with a wooden spatula. The Epoxybond Putty Resin and Hardener, System 3, are also mixed in equal parts by kneading and rolling in your hands until thoroughly mixed. The Epoxybond Resin White Finishing Paste may be added to System 2 in order to create System 4, a porcelainizing system.

making a mold for a missing part

1. Make a wax or plastic rubber mold of the missing part, such as your dentist uses.
2. Melt and stir waxes together, 2 parts beeswax to 1 part carnauba.
3. Pour into mold to harden.
4. Cement in place using Epoxyglass Resin and Epoxyglass Hardener as a cement mix.
5. Clamp or tape.
6. Let set and harden.
7. Trim away excess with razor blade or sharp knife.
8. Proceed as above with melted wax mix to finish.

This drawing shows the mold form of wax or plasticine used to take an impression of a handle for the opposite side of the vase. Note the nub ends that extend just below the lip edge of the cup and about halfway down.

9.   A metal tool kept warm by dipping in scalding water is good for molding the wax.

different kinds of damages*

Glaze damage.

A surface chip, sometimes called a flake chip or edge chip.

Damage to the edge called a lip chip.

*Note: Remove old material from any article that has been previously mended.

Backup support for a piece broken out of the edge of a plate is a double layer of masking tape folded over the heavy paste made of the filler mix.

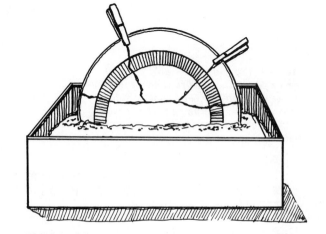

As illustrated by the plate in the sandbox, the lower half is bearing the weight of the upper pieces that are cemented in place and held by wooden clamp-type clothespins. The four edges have been cemented in a balanced position, and the entire plate is then placed on its lower edge deep in the sandbox for balance.

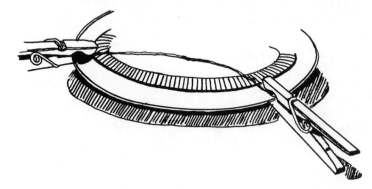

The plate at the right has been cemented and the parts are held together by clamp-type clothespins.

1. A small, surface flake damage to the glaze.
2. A surface flake that is called a chip, which includes glaze damage.
3. A chip that is out of an edge or one that is called a "lip chip," such as the edge of a drinking vessel, cup or glass.

"Edge chip" would be applied to a saucer or plate or the edge of any object to which we do not put our lips.

4. A broken-out piece.
5. An article broken in two or more pieces, such as a plate, a vase, or a lamp.
6. A broken base or pedestal.
7. A broken lid.
8. A broken finial to a lid.
9. A broken spout.
10. A broken handle.
11. A hairline crack.
12. Missing parts, such as heads, hands, legs, feet, wings, leaves, flowers, fruit, finials, knobs, handles, spouts, lids, and others too similar to mention.

how to use system 1, porcelainate, with other systems for mending, repairing, and restoring china

This material meets the need in mending for an acceptable substitute for porcelain. When the two-part Porcelainate system is compounded according to instructions, it simulates porcelain effectively. It is used to repair such damages to chinaware as these:

damage number 1: a surface flake damage to the glaze; china

step-by-step sequence

[1] Thoroughly clean and bleach, if necessary.

[2] Air dry.

[3] If surface flake damage has bitten down slightly into the china surface below, prepare Porcelainate Powder and Hardener, System 1, and make a firm paste. Color to match the article as required.

[4] Fill chip or flake using your finger or an art brush.

[5]   Permit material to get semi-hard, which it will do in 30 to 45 minutes.

[6]   Dampen fingers in water before material has set, and smooth away excess. Reduces need for sanding, and eliminates the scratching of surrounding areas of glaze.

[7]   If color matches surrounding area perfectly, apply final coat of New Gloss Glaze, System 5. If damaged area is deep, apply two or three thin layers of coating, permitting each layer to dry between coatings.

damage number 2:   surface or flake chip; china

HOW TO RESTORE A PLATE: The large chip or flake chip does not involve a broken edge. Mix Porcelainate Powder and Hardener (System 1) colored to match the hue of the plate. Apply to the damaged area. Let the mix harden overnight.

The result often of dishwashing accidents in which small pieces of a plate, saucer, cup, goblet, vase, or similar article is chipped from the front, but the damage does not go through to the back or underside, and the chipped-off piece is lost.

step-by-step sequence

[1]   Use electric handgrinder.

[2]   Cut a grid across the damaged area.

[3]   Clean off all residue and powder with cheesecloth rag dipped in lacquer thinner.

[4]   Air dry.

[5]   Prepare Porcelainate Powder and Hardener, and make a fairly firm paste. Color, if desirable.

[6]   Fill in chip or flake.

[7]   Use art brush to press into all crevices.

[8]   Dampen fingers in water, and smooth away excess. Reduces need for sanding.

[9]   If damaged area is deep, apply two or three thin layers.

[10]   Balance in sand box, and allow to dry between applications.

[11]   Sand gently until even with surrounding surface.

[12]   Match and mix final shade of paint color with New Gloss Glaze (boilproof).

[13]   Apply with brush.

[14]   Feather-out until the matching repair is invisibilized.

[15]   If color matches surrounding area perfectly, apply final coat of New Gloss Glaze (boilproof).

damage number 3: lip or edge chip; china

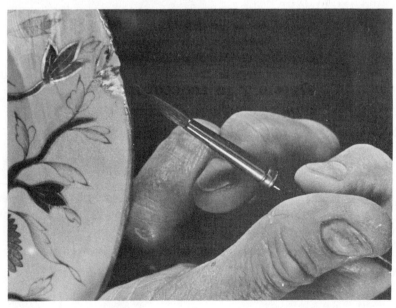

A lip chip plus a broken edge is called a lip or edge chip.

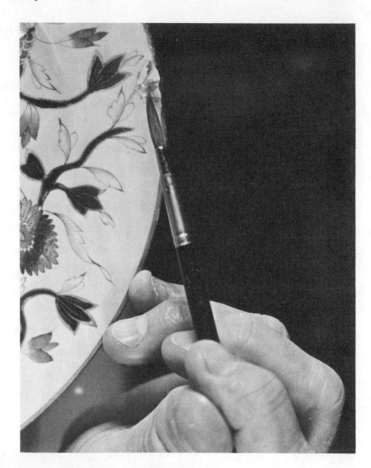

Paint in the flower decoration. Create and extend the design if necessary to match the colors and decoration and to cover the mend. Let the decoration dry. Glaze.

A broken-out edge chip or lip chip is a damage that occurs when one or two pieces in the shape of a "V" or wedge are broken in the side or lip edge of an article, and a backup support of masking tape is required.

step-by-step sequence

[1]   Use handgrinder to cut a grid, and even the edges in a "V" shape where the chip is broken out of the edge.

[2]   Apply masking tape across underside of open "V" area. Reinforce with Mortite or Plasticine to hold tape firm, because it may sag when filler is laid on it.

[3]   Clean off all residue and powder with cheesecloth rag dipped in lacquer thinner.

[4]   Air dry.

[5]   Perpare Porcelainate Powder and Hardener, and make a fairly firm paste. Color, if desirable.

[6]   Cement in the broken-out chip or flake.

[7]   Use art brush to press cement into all crevices.

[8]   Dampen fingers in water, and smooth away excess. **Reduces need for sanding.**

[9]   If damaged area is deep, apply two or three thin layers.

[10]   Balance in sand box, and allow to dry between applications.

[11]   Sand gently until even with surrounding surface.

[12]   Match and mix final shade of paint color with New Gloss Glaze (boilproof).

[13]   Apply with brush.

[14]   Feather-out until the matching repair is invisibilized.

damage number 4:
a broken-out piece; china

Cementing into place the broken out pieces of a small bowl or cup requires the sequencing shown above. Install each piece and secure with a bit of Scotch Tape. Number the pieces and tape into place. Once numbered in place, the tape is easily stripped off and the pieces reinstalled and cemented.

Retape each piece firmly in place to hold the pieces securely until the cement has had time to harden and dry. Remove the tape when the cement has hardened and proceed to porcelainize over the mend. Color, smooth, and blend to match surrounding areas, thus invisibilizing the mend.

This damage includes chips and pieces broken off plates and similar articles, also pieces broken off handles, spouts, the bottoms of cups, and other articles.

step-by-step sequence

[1]   Study the section or piece that needs to be restored. Cementing in the piece is only part of the problem. You are going to have to figure out how to anchor it, once you have made it.

[2]   First, use the following method if the piece to be restored has an irregular or jagged edge:

[3]   Turn the article around, and select an opposite section or piece that corresponds with the missing or broken-out piece in shape and design.

[4]   Apply molding rubber. Cover both sides of a larger area than the missing piece, so that the mold will have two sides, and the hollow will be a duplicate of the missing section or piece.

[5]   Plastic rubber mold will set in a few minutes. Follow directions given by the manufacturer.

[6]   If you are using wax, dip sheets of it in scalding water, and quickly mold it around the area of which you are making a model. As it cools, it will harden.

[7]   Remove mold carefully.

[8]   Trim excess by fittings. Try it over the missing section until you are satisfied with the duplication.

[9]   Mix just enough Porcelainate Powder and Hardener to fill mold.

[10]   Put it aside to set.

[11]   When the paste has hardened, remove, and discard the mold.

[12]   Use handgrinder to groove out corresponding channels in edges to be unified.

[13]   Fit the piece in until a snug fit is obtained.

[14]   Mix a fresh batch of Porcelainate, and cement into place by filling channels or grooves.

[15]   Dampen your fingers with water, and smooth away excess.

[16]   Apply tape to both sides of area if necessary, and set aside to harden.

[17]   When hard, complete painting and coloring to match surrounding area.

[18]   Glaze.

alternate step-by-step sequence (for irregular missing piece)

If your missing piece is small, say thumbnail size, proceed as follows:

[1]   Make a very firm Porcelainate mix.

[2]   Use handgrinder to channel-out a groove 1/4 inch deep all around the broken edges.

[3]   Press paste into the area to be filled.

[4]   Shape until you have exactly the size and shape needed.

[5]   Secure masking tape under the area to support the mold, and if necessary, firm this up with Mortite or Plasticine under the tape.

[6]   Balance in sandbox, and let harden.

[7]   When hard, grind off excess with hard rubber polishing disc.

[8]   Paint to match surrounding areas.

[9]   Glaze.

alternate step-by-step sequence (for missing piece that has no irregularity)

[1]   Place a slab of soft wax under the broken area, extending it beyond break on all sides.

[2]   Fold corners of wax up over edges away from missing area in order to secure wax trough. Let cool.

[3]   Secure with masking tape if necessary.

[4]   You now have a base on which to build in filler.

[5]   Make a firm paste of Porcelainate Powder and Hardener.

[6]   Smooth into area. Feather-out edges to exactly match and restore missing piece.

[7]   Dampen fingers in water and smooth away excess.

[8]   Set aside in sandbox to harden.

[9]   When hard, use soft rubber polishing wheel to polish off any unevenness, or sand down even with all edges. Use the fingernail test.

[10]   Decorate and glaze.

damage number 5: an article broken in two or more pieces; such as a a porcelain vase

A broken flower vase before mending. The broken out pieces may be numbered and taped into place. The tape is then removed, the pieces cemented into place, and the pieces retaped to hold them firmly and evenly until the cement has hardened.

A flower vase after mending. Excess cement must be removed; then the inside of the vase is reporcelainized and permitted to dry. Redecorating the outside can be accomplished by tracing off the design, taping carbon paper under the tracing paper, and transferring the missing design back onto the surface of the vase. The design can then be followed by using matching oil colors mixed with a bit of Glaze (System 5).

HOW TO MEND A PORCE-LAIN VASE AND RESTORE THE FLORAL DESIGN:

Step 1—The vase shown was broken in three fairly even pieces. However, had there been more pieces, these would first be numbered and installed by using Scotch Tape to secure each piece in place. Once numbered, remove tapes from these pieces and cement in place.

Step 2—The problem is to conceal the outside cracks which disfigure the vase. This is done by using tracing paper to trace off segments of the floral design. Then use Scotch Tape to secure carbon paper to the underside of the tracing paper and retrace the design on the vase, using a sharp, hard lead pencil. The design will transfer to the porcelain and needs only to be painted on. Mix the colors used with a touch of New Gloss Glaze for finish and hardener.

37

Step 3—In the vase shown, inside cracks appear.
These can be rendered invisible after mending by
porcelainizing (System 4).

step-by-step sequence

[1] Inspect damaged pieces for cracks and chips. These may be re-
     paired in accordance with procedures for same given under their
     respective headings.

[2] If your article is broken in more than three pieces, you will have
     to decide on its value to you. As far as mending is concerned, it
     may not be worth your time and the good materials it will take to
     restore it. A careful inspection will help you decide.

[3] Plan assembly of the broken pieces.

[4]   Prepare strips of masking tape in lengths needed to secure the pieces to be fitted into the article.

[5]   Prepare Porcelainate mix in equal parts.

[6]   Cement pieces into place in the article, secure with strips of masking tape from both the inside and the outside, and set aside to dry and harden.

[7]   Examine for uneven edges and displacement. The thickness of the material you use will determine the amount of displacement. If the pieces do not fit together perfectly, wait until paste has hardened, and grind off unevenness before removing masking tape.

[8]   Remove tapes.

[9]   If you have chips, you should use Porcelainate to fill them in, removing all excess.

[10]   Place in sandbox to dry and harden.

[11]   Sand smooth any remaining rough edges.

[12]   If you have to put on a broken handle, cement the pieces together. Let harden.

damage number 6:   a broken base or pedestal; china

step-by-step sequence

[1]   Inspect damage to the broken base for hairline cracks and chips.

[2]   If your article is broken in more than three pieces, you will have to decide on its value to you. As far as mending is concerned, unless it is an heirloom or wedding present, the time and good materials it will take to restore it may not be worthwhile. A careful inspection will help you decide.

[3]   Plan assembly of the broken pieces.

[4]   Prepare strips of masking tape in lengths needed to secure the pieces to be fitted into the article.

[5]   Prepare Porcelainate paste. Mix powder and hardener on two-to-one basis.

[6]   Cement pieces into place in the article, secure with strips of masking tape from both the inside and the outside as needed, and set aside to dry and harden.

[7] Examine for uneven edges and displacement. The thickness of the material you use will determine the amount of displacement. If the pieces do not fit together perfectly, wait until the cement has hardened, and grind off unevenness before removing masking tape.

[8] After grinding away ragged edges, reexamine for chips.

[9] Remove tapes.

[10] If you have chips, you should use Porcelainate mix to fill the chips in, removing all excess.

[11] Place in sandbox to dry and harden.

[12] Sand smooth any remaining rough edges.

[13] Prepare a slurry of System 1, and recoat the mended surfaces until the joins are invisibilized. Let harden.

[14] Now cream the remainder of the cement mix until it can be applied with a soft art brush.

[15] Apply creamy cement to the mended area, and blend it to a smooth join with handle and surrounding surfaces.

[16] Clean off excess. This is extremely important, because this clay cement mix will harden into a stone-hard substance, and once married to your article, is almost impossible to remove.

[17] Remove any rough edges with razor blade, and in a feathering-out motion, reblend cement with surrounding areas.

[18] Rebalance in sandbox, and let set and harden approximately 24 hours.

[19] When cement is beginning to dry and harden, remove with a razor blade any excess film left by cement on surrounding surfaces. You can get film off. Thick, hard stone will be virtually impossible to remove. There are ways, of course; you can use a hard rubber polishing disc in a handgrinder, or sandpaper. Sandpaper, however, is apt to scratch surrounding surfaces and do additional glaze damage.

[20] Prepare epoxy porcelainizing mix, and blend in oil color to match article. Porcelainize mended surfaces with System 4.

[21] Smooth until all edges and mends, as well as materials, are blended in with the body of the article.

[22] Set aside to dry for 24 to 36 hours.

[23] Decorate with oil paints and New Gloss Glaze.

[24] Finish glazing with New Gloss Glaze, System 5.

damage number 7:
a broken lid; porcelain

A broken soup tureen before repair, with multiple
breaks and chips, and the top ornamental finial broken off.

step-by-step sequence

[1]   Inspect damaged pieces of broken lid.

[2]   If the broken lid is chipped, cracked, and broken in more than
       three pieces, it may not be worth your time and the good ma-
       terials it will take to restore it. A careful inspection will help you
       decide.

[3]   Plan assembly of the broken pieces.

[4]   Prepare strips of masking tape in lengths needed to secure the
       pieces to be fitted into the article.

[5]   Prepare Porcelainate. Mix two parts to one.

[6]   Cement pieces into place, secure with strips of masking tape from
       both the inside and the outside, and set aside to dry and harden.

[7]   Examine for uneven edges and displacement. The thickness of the material you use will determine the amount of displacement. If the pieces do not fit together perfectly, wait until cement has hardened, and grind off unevenness before removing masking tape.

[8]   After grinding away ragged edges, reexamine for chips.

[9]   Remove tapes.

[10]   If you have chips, fill them in with the Porcelainate mix, removing all excess.

[11]   Place in sandbox or balance in a bed of wax to dry and harden.

[12]   Sand smooth any remaining rough edges.

[13]   If you have to put on a broken handle, cement the pieces together with Porcelainate mix. Let harden.

[14]   Grind a grid in the areas to be cemented together. You may put in a cross shape ("**X**") or, if it warrants it, a single groove.

[15]   The base cement should be firm. Press the cement into the grooves of the article's nubs and into the handle.

[16]   Apply tape to inside of the cover, and bring a long-enough piece of it out over the top to secure the handle in place.

[17]   Now cream the remainder of the mix until it can be applied with a soft art brush.

[18]   Apply creamy cement to the mended area, and blend it to a smooth join with handle and surrounding surfaces.

[19]   Clean off excess. This is extremely important, because this cement mix will harden into a stone-hard substance.

[20]   Remove any rough edges with razor blade, and in a feathering-out motion, reblend cement with surrounding areas.

[21]   Rebalance in wax bed or sandbox, and let set and harden for approximately 24 hours.

[22]   When cement is dry and hard, remove any excess film left by cement on surrounding surfaces.

[23]   Prepare a slurry of the epoxy mix, and blend in oil color to match the article. Porcelainize mended surfaces.

[24]   Smooth until all edges and mends, as well as materials, are blended in with the body of the server.

[25]   Set aside to dry for 24 to 36 hours.

[26]   Decorate with oil paints.

[27]   Finish glazing.

damage number 8:   a finial broken off a lid; porcelain or chinaware

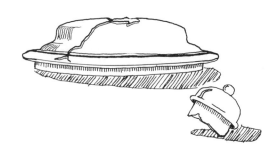

The broken lid is shown before repair with multiple breaks and chip. The finial or ornamental knob usually fixed to the top is also broken off, and a bad crack shows through the lid.

step-by-step sequence

[1]   The base cement should be firm. Press the cement into the grooves of the nubs and into the handle or finial.

[2]   Apply tape to inside of article, and bring a long-enough piece of it out over the edge to secure the handle in place.

[3]   Now cream the remainder of the cement mix until it can be applied with a soft art brush. Porcelainize surrounding surfaces.

[4]   Apply creamy cement to the mended area, and blend it to a smooth join with handle and surrounding surfaces in order to eliminate any hairline cracks. Clean off excess.

[5]   Glaze.

damage number 9:   a broken coffeepot spout; china

A coffeepot with a piece of the edging broken out of the pouring part of the spout.

HOW TO MEND A COFFEEPOT SPOUT:
Repair or working time is approximately 20
minutes. Step 1—Use System 3. Mix the
Epoxybond Putty Resin and Hardener 50/50
in sufficient quantity to build, shape, and
smooth-coat the mend.

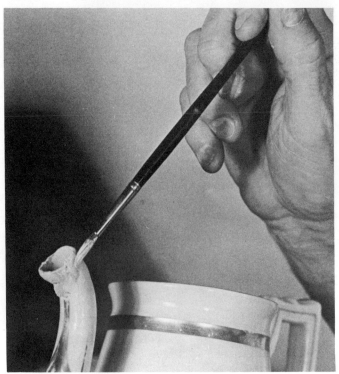

Step 2—Apply putty mix, press-
ing into ragged edges. Smooth
and shape. Let stand and harden.

44

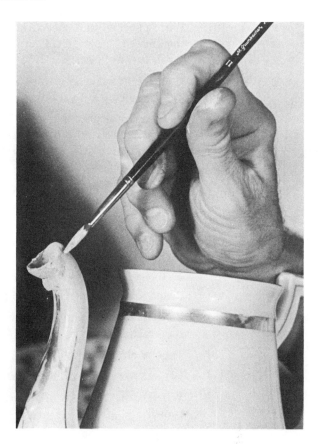

Step 3—Use System 4. Make a mix of the Epoxyglass Resin and Hardener, and add Epoxybond White Finishing Paste colored to match the piece being mended.

step-by-step sequence

[1]   First clean the pot thoroughly. Clean edges and surface to be restored. Boil in peroxide or washing soda to remove all stains. This will bleach out and reveal all spider cracks or other glaze damage.

[2]   Dry, and inspect damage for cracks extending from broken lip of spout down into pieces to be repaired.

[3]   Plan assembly of pieces.

[4]   Warm or oven-heat pieces to be cemented.

[5]   Prepare cement mix.

[6]   Prepare strips of masking tape in lengths needed to secure any pieces to be cemented together.

[7]   Grind away any ragged edges.

[8]   Now, if only the end or lip of the spout is broken off, grind in anchor grooves.

[9]   Where there is a deep crack extending from the break, grind along the line of the crack, decreasing the depth of the groove as the crack grows finer.

[10]   You are now ready to use cement mix to model and reshape the lip. Press clay into the line of the crack, and smooth away excess.

[11]   Form a lip or pouring spout with the cement mix, and model this carefully. Maintain in place, if necessary, with tape. Shape it as it was, and give it a slight trough in the middle to provide good pouring.

[12]   Keep smoothing and shaping the cement mix until you have restored the shape of the spout. Maintain in place with masking tape.

[13]   Now let us do a retake for a moment. If you have several pieces of broken spout, it will be necessary first to cement them together.

[14]   Prepare cement mix in equal parts.

[15]   Cement all pieces together working from the largest two down to the smallest.

[16]   Tape each set to maintain adjustment of edges.

[17]   Let set for 24 hours. Remove tapes.

[18]   When dry, remove all excess with a razor blade (single-edge type).

[19]   Clean.

[20]   Complete cementing process until all pieces are recemented to reform the broken spout.

[21]   Balance in sandbox until dry.

[22]   Cement into place on pot, and again balance and dry in sandbox. Remove all tapes when mend is dry.

[23]   Proceed as in Steps 7 through 12.

[24]   Now for the finish. Prepare a mix of Epoxyglass Resin and Hardener in equal parts, blend in Epoxybond White Finishing Paste, and mix with color to shade required to match pot.

[25]   Apply with a feathering-out motion. Smooth and blend this porcelainizing material in an outward motion. Down stroke, and add covering material as needed until all signs of the mending job have disappeared completely. You may have to cover the entire spout. Be sure to go down through the open lip with an art brush to cover all signs of the hardened clay-mending material.

[26]   When satisfied that you have invisibilized the **mend**, set in sand-box to dry for at least 24 hours.

[27]   Decorate in accordance with motif on pot, or create a new one. Use oil paints mixed with New Gloss Glaze.

[28]   Glaze with New Gloss Glaze. Use a camel's-hair brush to apply. Do not use a spray glaze.

[29]   Apply gold decoration to spout as the last decorating step. If you are using art gold in the paste form, apply carefully as directed on package.

damage number 10:   a cup with a broken handle; china

The drawing at the left shows a broken handle opposite remaining nubs on the cup. The clay mixture can be hand rolled to the desired shape and thinness or thickness, and then applied. See procedures on how to replace a missing handle or one so badly broken it is not worth saving. The drawing at the right shows the handle applied and the repair made invisible. See procedures for invisibilizing.

For a cup with a handle broken in two pieces (left), mending must rejoin the handle to a section that is also broken out of the cup. The nub left on the back of the cup (far right) forms a base on which to mold or rebuild the handle. The handle for a cup resembles a "5"; when molding a handle, always keep a figure "5" in mind.

step-by-step sequence

[1]   Study the article. Make a mold if you have to.

[2]   Use grinder to trench out grooves in the nubs left where the handle broke off.

[3]   Grind out similar grooves in the broken pieces of the handle (if more than one piece).

[4]   Use Porcelainate mix to cement broken pieces together (handle only).

[5]   When handle is whole, apply to cup, or gravy boat or tureen or pitcher or pot, or whatever.

[6]   Cement the two articles together by filling the grooves with the mix, and make sure that the edges fit together perfectly.

[7]   Use a metal clamp or tape. (A word about how to tape: Go to the inside of the article, secure the tape, bring it out over the rim, and secure it to the handle lengthwise. Fasten end to bottom of the article.)

[8]   If piece is heavy, and there is too much strain on handle, reinforce as follows: Beg some old or used drills from your dentist. Use grinder as a drill. Drill 1/2 inch holes in the ends of the handle and through the nubs into the interior of the article.

[9]   Fill both holes in the handle with paste mix.

[10]   Insert end pieces of aluminum wire. (Same procedure can be used to piece broken pieces of handle together).

[11]   Let handle set and dry.

[12]   Insert wired ends of handle through holes in the nubs of the article. Bend in opposite directions until tight.

[13]   Fill holes and grooves with Porcelainate mix.

[14]   Tape over to firmly secure handle.

[15]   Also tape from inside, and bring out over handle length-wise. Secure end of tape to bottom of article.

[16]   Allow to set.

[17]   When hard, remove tapes, and prepare for next step by smoothing away any excess. Use grinder and hard rubber polishing wheel.

[18]   Prepare equal parts of Epoxyglass Resin and Hardener with Epoxybond Resin (White Finishing Paste). Add color until the entire mix is the exact shade required to match your article.

[19]   Apply this mix with an art brush until all edges and surfaces are

perfectly blended, both on the inside as well as on the outside of the mends. Use this mix to cover over the clay and wire on the inside. This mix will harden into a porcelain-like substance that matches your article. And, of course, it is unaffected by washing.

[20]   Feather-out this mix wherever applied until you have a perfect blend.

[21]   Set aside to dry in sandbox.

[22]   Glaze and decorate.

[23]   After glazing, apply art gold decoration if required.

[24]   Air dry and reglaze if you have not used gold decoration. (The glaze will turn gold black.) So, gold, *last* always.

damage number 11: cracks and fractures; china plate

HOW TO RESTORE A PLATE WITH FRACTURES AND HAIRLINE CRACKS: Repair time is 10 minutes; bleaching time is 24 to 48 hours.

Step 1—Place plate in a plastic pan. Pour pure bleach over the plate until it is covered. Let the plate soak until the cracks disappear.

Step 2—Remove the plate from the plastic pan; wash and dry thoroughly.

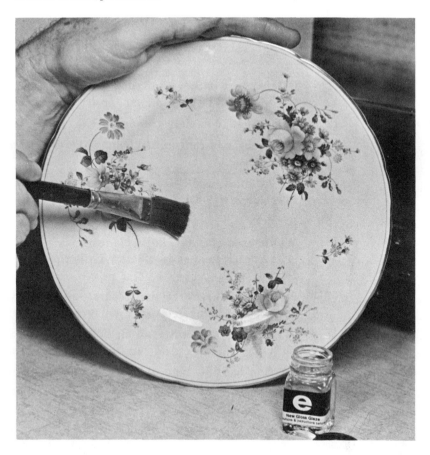

Step 3—Brush on a coat of Glaze (System 5) or spray with acrylic lacquer. NOTE: Lacquer will not hold up but will peel off after a few washings; New Gloss Glaze will not peel off.

A chinaware article that has been cracked or fractured requires careful examination.

statement of the problem

Getting ready to boil your cracked article: First, examine the edges. Are the edges of the crack tight together, or can you insert a razor blade between them? Is the crack dirty, or are the edges aged and yellowed or discolored? Whether the edges are tight together or loose, boil out any possible discoloration and dirt. Use an enamel pan or bucket big-enough and deep-enough to enable you to submerge the article. The cracked part must be completely covered. After the crack is truly clean and seems to have disappeared, air dry it, and treat the crack as follows:

step-by-step sequence

[1]   **Determine whether the crack is tight or loose, that is, whether the edges can be spread apart or are immovable.**

[2]   **Boil article; completely immerse the cracks; use a safe bleach.**

[3]   **Reinspect, and continue to boil until truly clean with all discoloration gone.**

[4]   **A few minutes before end of boil, prepare two-to-one parts of Porcelainate Powder and Hardener into paste.**

[5]   **Air dry.**

[6]   **While warm, insert a knife blade or razor's edge into the open end of the crack to open it wider. Wiggle the blade in. Do not press or force it in.**

[7]   **Now press the Porcelainate paste into the crack. Use a wooden spatula (a tongue depressor will do).**

[8]   **Smooth paste evenly, and clean off excess; press in the cement. Moisten your fingers as you work to press in the cement.**

[9]   **Feather-out the edge until all surplus is removed and the filling is even with the adjoining surfaces.**

[10]   **Dry for several hours.**

[11]   **When dry, decorate or glaze.**

Now we have a few ifs:

If the article is porcelain and *not* more than 1/16 inch thick, and *if* the crack is tight, you have repaired the crack by the above steps.

If your article is porcelain and *more* than 1/16 inch in thickness, you will have to use a handgrinder to make an "X" at the opening of the crack: On the underside, if a plate; on the inside, if a cup. If any case, make a "X" where least observable and where you *know* you are going to have to decorate or porcelainize over it. This is not difficult, it is just another step.

If the crack is mere surface damage or the entire surface is crazed, that is, covered with a fine, hairline network of surface cracks and discoloration:

1.   Boil as previously instructed until cracks become invisible.

2.   Air dry, and repair as indicated above.

shock from extreme change of temperature in air or water may cause damage.

Glass cannot be added to glass to make a repair, because it would take molten glass to do it. Molten glass cannot be added to cool glass, because of the shock of temperature change to both the hot and cold glass. Glass-like china is made at high temperatures and cannot be subjected to heat again unless very gradually.

System 2, Epoxyglass Resin and Hardener mix, is used to repair such damages to glass as these:

damage numbers 1 & 2:
surface and flake damage;
glass (snuff bottles)

The flake damage on the left of the Pekin glass snuff bottle (far left) was restored with a single application or Epoxyglass Resin and Hardener. Two jade snuff bottles are shown on the right. The surface damage on the right of the far right bottle was restored with a single application of Epoxyglass Resin and Hardener.

These are the types of damages that do not cut through to the bottom, and include small pieces of a goblet, vase, plate, or similar article chipped off the top surface and lost. While damage to a glass article is similar to that of a china article, the mending system is entirely dfferent.

step-by-step sequence

[1]   **Mix Epoxyglass Resin and Epoxyglass Hardener in equal parts. Color can be added if necessary.**

3.   Apply New Gloss Glaze (boilproof) with a suitable artist brush in easy stages.

4.   Overlay with succeeding coats, each thicker than the previous coat until you are satisfied that the article has been restored to its original luster, brilliance, and gloss.

damage number 12:
missing parts; china

A missing handle can be replaced in two ways. One is by making a mix and casting Porcelainate and Hardener in a mold. The correct size can be taken from a like handle, or measured, or done by eye, by comparison with similar pieces or pictures, or by experience. The second method is by hand alone.

Shown above is a coffeepot with a missing handle and a broken out section.

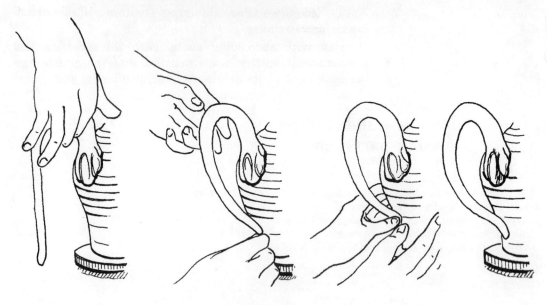

HOW TO MAKE AND APPLY A HANDLE: Step 1—Join the top end with your mix of Epoxybond Putty Resin and Hardener and smooth. Step 2—Now join the bottom end of the handle to your item. Step 3—Press with your fingers to a set and smooth your join. Step 4—Leave your finger marks as your brand of decoration or identification.

step-by-step sequence (damages, missing parts)

[1] Classify damage (flake chip, lip or edge chip, missing part, crack, or multiple breaks).

[2] Clean all surfaces thoroughly. Boil to loosen all foreign substances, old glue, or old mending materials.

[3] If you have to make a mold for a missing part, heat or warm until pliable a sheet of wax, and a mold. Or:

[4] Use plastic mold. Mix according to directions, equal parts; let set for about 8 minutes on the area of which you are making an impression. Remove, and fill the mold with cement mixture; color may be added to match the color of the article you are mending. Also, mix color into Porcelainate and Hardener very gradually to get a smooth blend.

[5] Fill the mold with the mixture; set aside to harden 24 to 36 hours.

[6] When molded material is hard, remove from mold, and smooth

edges with carbide rubber wheel set in a handgrinder. Cemen[t] place. Use masking tape for support or a wax mold for backu[p] hold material in place while mending-cement is hardening.

[7] Apply one or two coats of New Gloss Glaze to mended area[.] set and dry.

[8] Remove tapes and/or wax back-up support. Smooth with rubber disc. Apply one or two coats of New Gloss Glaze.

[9] Make a mix of System 4. Add color to match article. Get [a] shade by matching in daylight. Coat mended areas with Porcelainizing mix. Feather-out the epoxy cement until it i[s] fectly blended with all surrounding areas.

[10] Reglaze with New Gloss Glaze. Set aside to cure, and whe[n] and hard, decorate to design. Gold after glaze. Glaze spray[ed] top of gold will turn it a bronze cast.

how to use system 2 with other systems for mending, repairing, and restoring glass

Glass is not repairable with glass, but it can be beau[tifully] mended. The original usefulness may not be entirely restor[ed] with the right materials and techniques for repairing the d[amage] the repair can be made a practicable matter and almost un[notice]able.

The techniques for restoring glass are no differe[nt from] those used to mend an article of chinaware, perhaps beca[use the] object is the same, but the approach may vary in any give[n mend]ing problem. After all, the problem in every case is to m[ake the] repair and then finish it, so that it matches as closely as [possible] the surrounding surfaces of the article. Damages to cle[ar glass] complicate the problem of concealment.

Just about the same kinds of damage occur to gla[ss as] china. They are classified as flake chips, rim or lip chips, [missing] parts, and multiple breaks. Glass does not suffer glaze da[mage as] it is not glazed, but it is easily chipped; some glass artic[les have] edges that are apt to suffer damage more quickly tha[n other] articles, and the base of a glass article usually needs grea[ter care] and protection from sudden shock.

Glass can withstand great pressure, but a sudden [blow]

[2]   Secure *Scotch Tape* to each side, top and bottom, to form a channel or "footer" into which you can drip the material, drop by drop, until the channel has been filled. Never mind unevenness, because this can be ground smooth later, and glaze applied. The glaze will eradicate any scratches from grinding, polishing, and smoothing.

[3]   Using a brush, fill in the flake or chip, drop by drop.

[4]   Allow time for hardening (24 hours), balancing the article in sandbox. Be careful to keep grains of sand away from mending material during this quick-drying, long-hardening process.

[5]   When the mending material is dry and hard, remove with a razor blade any excess film on surrounding areas. Mere film also comes off easily by using a small wad of cheesecloth dipped or dampened in lacquer thinner. Mended surfaces must be ground smooth. Use a handgrinder and light grinding stone or carborundum wheel to even out surfaces and match surrounding areas. Scratches and abrasions will appear. These are quickly eliminated after grinding by applying a second coat of Epoxyglass Resin and Epoxyglass Hardener mix. Allow time to dry (30 to 45 minutes) and coat New Gloss Glaze, System 5.

[6]   Apply final New Gloss Glaze coating as necessary.

damage number 3: broken out edge chip or lip chip; glass

HOW TO RESTORE A GLASS WITH A PIECE MISSING: Step 1—Shown is a wineglass with a piece missing.

Step 2—For mending glass, mix Epoxyglass Resin and Hardener 50/50. Color slightly with blue if glass is lead crystal or with green if glass is not lead crystal. This gives your epoxy a crystalline quality and will defer eventual yellowing of the material. Set aside mix while preparing the glass for the mend. Working time is 15 to 20 minutes; curing time is 24 to 48 hours. CAUTION: After the mend is finished, do not use energine or acetone to clean the glass. Merely wash fingerprints off in warm, clear, sudsy water. Or thoroughly clean the glass while still in the mending process, carefully removing all spots and excess material with a razor blade and acetone or lacquer thinner.

Step 3—Create a wall of Scotch Tape on the inside and outside where the piece is missing. Do not let the two pieces of tape get stuck together.

Step 4—Use camel's hair or acrylic bristle brush and drip epoxy mix in the opening. Set aside; let harden.

Step 5—Remove tapes. Smooth and clean off excess with a razor blade dampened in lacquer thinner.

Step 6—Coat with a second coat of epoxy mix. Set aside to harden. Hardening time is 8 minutes.

Step 7—Coat with New Gloss Glaze for an almost invisible mend.

3.   Apply New Gloss Glaze (boilproof) with a suitable artist brush in easy stages.

4.   Overlay with succeeding coats, each thicker than the previous coat until you are satisfied that the article has been restored to its original luster, brilliance, and gloss.

damage number 12: missing parts; china

A missing handle can be replaced in two ways. One is by making a mix and casting Porcelainate and Hardener in a mold. The correct size can be taken from a like handle, or measured, or done by eye, by comparison with similar pieces or pictures, or by experience. The second method is by hand alone.

Shown above is a coffeepot with a missing handle and a broken out section.

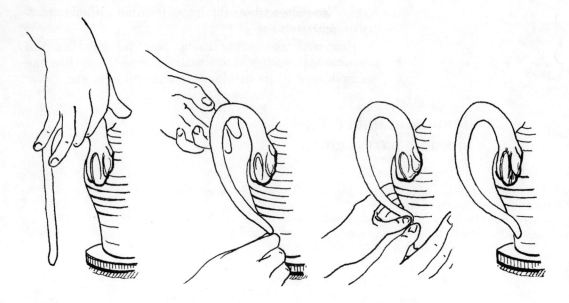

*HOW TO MAKE AND APPLY A HANDLE: Step 1—Join the
top end with your mix of Epoxybond Putty Resin and Hardener
and smooth. Step 2—Now join the bottom end of the handle
to your item. Step 3—Press with your fingers to a set
and smooth your join. Step 4—Leave your finger marks as
your brand of decoration or identification.*

step-by-step sequence
(damages, missing parts)

[1]   Classify damage (flake chip, lip or edge chip, missing part, crack, or multiple breaks).

[2]   Clean all surfaces thoroughly. Boil to loosen all foreign substances, old glue, or old mending materials.

[3]   If you have to make a mold for a missing part, heat or warm until pliable a sheet of wax, and a mold. Or:

[4]   Use plastic mold. Mix according to directions, equal parts; let set for about 8 minutes on the area of which you are making an impression. Remove, and fill the mold with cement mixture; color may be added to match the color of the article you are mending. Also, mix color into Porcelainate and Hardener very gradually to get a smooth blend.

[5]   Fill the mold with the mixture; set aside to harden 24 to 36 hours.

[6]   When molded material is hard, remove from mold, and smooth

edges with carbide rubber wheel set in a handgrinder. **Cement in place. Use masking tape for support or a wax mold for backup to hold material in place while mending-cement is hardening.**

[7]   **Apply one or two coats of New Gloss Glaze to mended area. Let set and dry.**

[8]   **Remove tapes and/or wax back-up support. Smooth with soft rubber disc. Apply one or two coats of New Gloss Glaze.**

[9]   **Make a mix of System 4. Add color to match article. Get exact shade by matching in daylight. Coat mended areas with this Porcelainizing mix. Feather-out the epoxy cement until it is perfectly blended with all surrounding areas.**

[10]   **Reglaze with New Gloss Glaze. Set aside to cure, and when dry and hard, decorate to design. Gold after glaze. Glaze sprayed on top of gold will turn it a bronze cast.**

how to use system 2
with other systems for
mending, repairing, and
restoring glass

Glass is not repairable with glass, but it can be beautifully mended. The original usefulness may not be entirely restored, but with the right materials and techniques for repairing the damage, the repair can be made a practicable matter and almost unnoticeable.

The techniques for restoring glass are no different from those used to mend an article of chinaware, perhaps because the object is the same, but the approach may vary in any given mending problem. After all, the problem in every case is to make the repair and then finish it, so that it matches as closely as possible the surrounding surfaces of the article. Damages to clear glass complicate the problem of concealment.

Just about the same kinds of damage occur to glass as to china. They are classified as flake chips, rim or lip chips, missing parts, and multiple breaks. Glass does not suffer glaze damage as it is not glazed, but it is easily chipped; some glass articles have edges that are apt to suffer damage more quickly than china articles, and the base of a glass article usually needs greater care and protection from sudden shock.

Glass can withstand great pressure, but a sudden blow or

shock from extreme change of temperature in air or water may cause damage.

Glass cannot be added to glass to make a repair, because it would take molten glass to do it. Molten glass cannot be added to cool glass, because of the shock of temperature change to both the hot and cold glass. Glass-like china is made at high temperatures and cannot be subjected to heat again unless very gradually.

System 2, Epoxyglass Resin and Hardener mix, is used to repair such damages to glass as these:

damage numbers 1 & 2:
surface and flake damage;
glass (snuff bottles)

The flake damage on the left of the Pekin glass snuff bottle (far left) was restored with a single application or Epoxyglass Resin and Hardener. Two jade snuff bottles are shown on the right. The surface damage on the right of the far right bottle was restored with a single application of Epoxyglass Resin and Hardener.

These are the types of damages that do not cut through to the bottom, and include small pieces of a goblet, vase, plate, or similar article chipped off the top surface and lost. While damage to a glass article is similar to that of a china article, the mending system is entirely dfferent.

step-by-step sequence

[1]   Mix Epoxyglass Resin and Epoxyglass Hardener in equal parts. Color can be added if necessary.

This is the type of damage that goes through from one side to the other of goblets, vases, and similar articles, and occurs when "V" or wedge-shaped pieces are broken out in washing and are lost. Here again, *Scotch Tape* rather than masking tape is used as back-up support for this type of mend on glass.

step-by-step sequence

[1]   Carefully apply *Scotch Tape* across both sides of the open "V" area to make a trough between.

[2]   Mix equal parts of Epoxyglass Resin and Epoxyglass Hardener.

[3]   Using brush, drip the mixture into the trough until it has been filled.

[4]   Set aside to harden for at least 24 hours.

[5]   After tape has been removed, use a razor blade or handgrinder (carborundum cutting disc) lightly to remove excess material.

[6]   Apply a second coating of Epoxyglass Resin and Epoxyglass Hardener mix to eradicate any scratches that may appear from grinding.

[7]   Apply New Gloss Glaze as in preceding procedure.

damage number 4:   restoring a missing or broken out piece; glass

When restoring a missing or broken out piece too large to be called a chip (a piece that is a part of the structural body of the article), a new piece may be constructed with Epoxyglass Resin and Epoxyglass Hardener mix, cast, and then permitted to harden in a mold. The new piece is permanently affixed to the article.

step-by-step sequence

[1]   Study the section or missing piece which needs to be restored. Making the missing piece is only part of the problem. You are going to have to figure out how to anchor it once you have made it.

[2]   First, use the following method if the piece to be restored has an irregular or jagged edge.

[3]   Turn the article around, and select an opposite section or piece that corresponds with the missing piece in shape and design.

[4]   Apply molding rubber. Cover both sides of an area larger than the missing piece, so that the mold will have two sides, and the hollow will be a duplicate of the missing section or piece.

[5]   Plastic rubber mold will set in a few minutes. Follow instructions given by the manufacturer.

[6]   If you are using wax, dip sheets of it in scalding hot water and quickly mold it around the area of which you are making a mold. As it cools, it will harden.

[7]   Remove mold carefully.

[8]   Trim excess by fittings. Try it over the missing section until you just about have the size mold for exact duplication.

[9]   Mix just-enough Epoxyglass Resin and Epoxyglass Hardener in equal parts to fill the mold.

[10]   Put it aside to set.

[11]   When the putty has hardened, remove, and discard the mold.

[12]   Use handgrinder to groove out corresponding channels in edges to be unified.

[13]   Fit in the new piece until a snug fit is obtained.

[14]   Mix a fresh supply of Epoxyglass Resin and Epoxyglass Hardener, and cement into place by filling channels or grooves.

[15]   Dampen fingers with lacquer thinner, and smooth away excess.

[16]   Apply tape to both sides of area, if necessary, and set aside to harden.

[17]   When hard, complete any painting and coloring that may be necessary.

[18]   Glaze.

damage number 5: surface damage to a lamp or similar article; glass

To repair a lamp, dismantle it completely. If it is on a base and can be removed, take it off. The lamp must be taken apart— and this means removing the shade, harp, electric wiring, bolts, and everything else. This must be done in order to mend the structural glass.

step-by-step sequence

[1]   Classify damage (flake chip, lip or edge chip, missing part, crack, or multiple breaks).

[2]   Clean all surfaces thoroughly. Boil to loosen all foreign substances, old glue, or old mending materials.

[3]   If you have to make a mold for a missing part, heat or warm until pliable a sheet of wax, and make a mold. Or:

[4]   If you prefer using plastic molding material, mix according to directions, equal parts, and let set for about 8 minutes on the area of which you are making an impression. Remove, and fill the mold with cement mixture.

[5]   Fill mold, and set aside to harden overnight.

[6]   When molded material is hard, smooth edges with carbide rubber wheel set in a handgrinder. Cement in place. Use masking tape or a wax back-up mold to hold in place while repair cement is hardening.

[7]   Apply one or two coats of New Gloss Glaze. Let dry. Recoat with Epoxyglass Resin and Epoxyglass Hardener mix. Feather-out this mix until it is perfectly blended with surrounding surfaces.

[8]   Reglaze repaired area with New Gloss Glaze. This substance can be feathered-out. The repair should be invisible or almost. In any case, it will be as near perfect as is professionally possible.

damage number 6: a broken
base of an article; glass

step-by-step sequence

[1]   Use, but only if absolutely necessary, handgrinder and carborundum disc (made of diamond dust). Warming pieces first, place the article under faucet drip of warm water, and grind in anchor grooves. If you grind, your mend will show.

[2]   To make a mold for a missing part or bare damage with multiple breaks, heat sheet wax, and make a mold.

[3]   Clean the surfaces of the damaged pieces.

[4]   Apply mold material. If you use plastic mold, mixture should be made of equal parts.

[5]   Apply plastic mix with a spatula, permitting time of 8 minutes.

[6]   Prepare Epoxyglass Resin and Epoxyglass Hardener mix. Fill the mold with mixture. Permit to harden.

[7]   Remove molded piece, and cement into place with additional epoxy mixture.

[8]   The repaired area can be glazed with a coat of New Gloss Glaze. When it is dry, additional thin coats of epoxy mix may be added with a feathering-out motion.

[9]   Dampen your fingers first in solvent and then in the epoxy mix to perfect this feathering-out technique.

damage number 7: a broken lid with a broken finial; glass

step-by-step sequence

[1]   Prepare strips of masking tape in lengths needed to secure the piece or pieces to be fitted into the article.

[2]   Prepare Epoxyglass Resin and Epoxyglass Hardener mix in equal parts.

[3]   Cement finial into place on the lid, and secure with strips of masking tape. Set aside to dry and harden.

[4]   Examine for uneven edges and displacement. The thickness of the material you use will determine the amount of displacement. If the pieces do not fit together perfectly, wait until cement has hardened, warm the pieces, and polish off unevenness before removing masking tape.

[5]   After polishing away ragged edges, reexamine for chips.

[6]   Remove tapes.

[7]   If you have chips, use a thick mix of Epoxyglass Resin and Epoxyglass Hardener to fill the chips in, one layer at a time. Remove excess.

[8]   Place in sandbox or wax bed to dry and harden.

[9]   The Epoxyglass Resin and Epoxyglass Hardener mix should be thick. Apply the mix with an art brush to get into the breaks of the nubs of the article and into the finial.

[10]   Now remove excess cement. If you need more, you can apply it evenly all around the mend with a soft art brush dipped in thinner.

[11]   Clean off excess. This is extremely important, because this epoxy

mix will harden into a glass-like substance, and once married to the article, is almost impossible to remove without damage to the appearance of the mend.

[12]　　Remove any rough edges by adding a thin coat of the epoxy mix in a feathering-out motion. Reblend mix with surrounding areas.

[13]　　Rebalance in sandbox or wax bed, and allow to set and harden (approximately 24 hours).

[14]　　When epoxy cement is dry and hard, remove with a razor blade any excess film left by cement on surrounding surfaces. The film will come off, but thick, hard epoxy cement will be virtually impossible to remove or polish without spoiling the appearance. There are ways, of course. Keep your work to a fine finish at each stage as you go. You may remedy bad effects with New Gloss Glaze, but this is a remedy, not a cure.

[15]　　To decorate or porcelainize Pyrex, Milkglass, or Corning Ware, prepare Epoxyglass Resin and Epoxyglass Hardener mix, and blend in oil color to match article. Apply this to mended surfaces.

[16]　　Smooth with fingers dipped in solvent until all edges and mends, as well as materials, are blended in with the body of the article.

[17]　　Set aside to dry for 24 to 36 hours.

[18]　　Decorate with oil paints and New Gloss Glaze.

[19]　　Apply final coating of New Gloss Glaze.

damage number 8:　a hole in the side of a vase; glass

step-by-step sequence

[1]　　If the vase is large enough for your hand to be inserted inside, apply *Scotch Tape* or masking tape over the hole from the inside.

[2]　　Surround the outside area with soft wax to the depth needed, and fill the hole with System 2 mix, being sure to keep the article placed in the sandbox so that the area being mended is right-side up. This will prevent the mending material from running out of the mold.

[3]　　If the vase is too small for you to work with your fingers from the inside, you can use the wooden handle of a brush or the handle of an ordinary kitchen bottle cleaner.

[4]　　Attach the tape very lightly to the end of the handle, and ease

it into the vase, smoothing it against the sides of the broken-out area.

[5]   Anchor the tape well beyond the hole, beginning at the bottom.

[6]   Use another layer of backup tape if needed.

[7]   Fill the hole with the Epoxyglass Resin and Epoxyglass Hardener mix, and leave article balanced in sandbox to prevent loss of material.

[8]   Allow from 24 to 36 hours for drying and curing.

[9]   In filling a hole of this kind, it may be well to heat the epoxy mix first in order to hasten the hardening time and to prevent the mix from being runny.

[10]   Another precaution: Use *Scotch Tape* over the filled hole. Do not use masking tape, because it will leave a rough surface. Use tape to support and hold material in place while hardening.

[11]   When dry and hard (24 to 36 hours), remove tapes, and smooth surfaces with razor blade or handgrinder.

[12]   Apply one or two coats of New Gloss Glaze.

[13]   If glass is colored, add color to material prior to filling the hole, and match the material to the article by matching exact shade in daylight.

[14]   Coat surrounding surfaces of mended article by perfectly matching epoxy mix. Feather-out material by spreading or thinning it. Keep fingers dampened in lacquer thinner while stroking, spreading, and feathering-out to the finest edges.

damage number 9:
a broken spout; glass

step-by-step sequence

[1]   Inspect damaged pieces for cracks and chips. These will have to be repaired in accordance with procedures for same given under their respective headings.

[2]   If your article has multiple breaks and is chipped besides, you will have to decide on its value to you. As far as mending is concerned, it may not be worth your time and the good materials it will take to restore it. A careful inspection will help you decide.

[3]   Plan assembly of the broken glass pieces.

[4]   Prepare strips of masking tape in lengths needed to secure the pieces to be fitted into the item.

[5]   Prepare cement mix in equal parts.

[6]   Cement pieces into place in the item, secure with strips of masking tape from both the inside and the outside, and set aside to dry and harden.

[7]   Examine for uneven edges and displacement. The thickness of the material you use will determine the amount of displacement. If the pieces do not fit together perfectly, wait until cement has hardened, warm the pieces, and polish off unevenness before removing masking tape.

[8]   After polishing away ragged edges, reexamine for chips.

[9]   Remove tapes.

[10]   If you have chips, you should use a thick epoxy cement mix of equal parts to fill the chips in, one layer at a time. Remove all excess.

[11]   Place in sandbox or wax bed to dry and harden.

[12]   Polish any remaining rough edges smooth with a soft rubber disc.

[13]   If you have to put on a broken handle, cement the pieces together. Let harden.

[14]   Warm pieces to be cemented.

[15]   The epoxy cement should be thick. Apply the cement with an art brush to get into the breaks of the article's nubs and into the handle.

[16]   Apply tape to inside of article, and bring a long-enough piece of it out over the edge to secure the handle in place.

[17]   Now remove excess. If you need more epoxy, apply it evenly all around the mend with a soft brush dipped in thinner.

[18]   As you apply the cement to the mended area, blend it with thinner until you obtain a smooth join with handle and surrounding surfaces.

[19]   Clean off excess. This is extremely important, because this epoxy cement mix will harden into a glass-like substance, and once married to your article, is almost impossible to remove without damage to appearance.

[20]   Remove any rough edges by adding a thin coat of epoxy cement, and in a feathering-out motion, reblend with surrounding areas.

[21]   Rebalance in sandbox or wax bed, and let set and harden for approximately 24 hours.

[22]   When epoxy cement is dry and hard, remove with a razor blade any excess film left by cement on surrounding surfaces. You can

get film off. A thick, hard epoxy will be virtually impossible to remove or polish without damage to appearance. There are ways, of course; but try to keep your work to a fine finish at each stage as you go. You may remedy bad effects with glaze, but it is a remedy, not a cure.

[23]   To decorate or porcelainize milkglass, prepare epoxy porcelainizing mix, and blend in oil color to match article. Apply to mended surfaces.

[24]   Smooth until all edges and mends, as well as materials, are blended in with the body of the article.

[25]   Set aside to dry for 24 to 36 hours.

[26]   Decorate with oil paints and glaze.

[27]   Finish glazing with New Gloss Glaze.

damage number 10: a broken handle; glass

step-by-step sequence

[1]   Inspect damaged pieces for any additional damage. These may be repaired in accordance with procedures for same given under their respective headings.

[2]   If your article has a broken handle and is chipped, cracked, and broken in more than three pieces, you will have to decide on its value to you. As far as mending is concerned, it may not be worth your time and the good materials it will take to restore it. A careful inspection will help you decide.

[3]   Plan assembly of the broken pieces.

[4]   Prepare strips of masking tape in lengths needed to secure the pieces to be fitted into the article.

[5]   Prepare cement mix in equal parts.

[6]   Cement pieces into place in the article, secure with strips of masking tape from both the inside and the outside, and set aside to dry and harden.

[7]   Examine for uneven edges and displacement. The thickness of the material you use will determine the amount of displacement.

[8]   If the pieces do not fit together perfectly, wait until cement has hardened, and grind off unevenness before removing masking tape.

[9]   **Remove tapes.**

[10]   **If you have chips, you should use System 2 to fill them in, removing all excess.**

[11]   **Place in sandbox to dry and harden.**

[12]   **Sand smooth any remaining rough edges.**

[13]   **If you have to put on a broken handle, cement the pieces together. Let harden.**

[14]   **Grind a grid in the top and bottom nubs on the article, and grind grooves in top and bottom of handle. You can put in a cross shape ("X") or a single groove.**

[15]   **The base cement should begin to set before using. Press the cement into the grooves of the article's nubs and into the handle.**

[16]   **Apply tape to inside of article, and bring a long-enough piece of it out over the edge to secure the handle in place.**

[17]   **Now thin the remainder of the mix until it can be applied with a soft art brush.**

[18]   **Apply cement to the mended area, and blend it to a smooth join with handle and surrounding surfaces.**

[19]   **Clean off excess. This is extremely important, because this cement mix will harden into a glass-hard substance, and once married to your article, is almost impossible to remove.**

[20]   **Remove any rough edges with razor blade, and in a feathering-out motion, reblend cement with surrounding areas.**

[21]   **Rebalance in sandbox, and let set and harden approximately 24 hours.**

[22]   **When cement is dry and hard, remove with a razor blade any excess film left by cement on surrounding surfaces. Film you can get off. Thick, hard cement will be virtually impossible to remove. There are ways, of course; you can use a hard rubber polishing disc in a handgrinder, or sandpaper. Sandpaper, however, is apt to scratch surrounding surfaces and do additional glaze damage.**

[23]   **Prepare epoxy mix, blend in oil color to match article, and recoat mended surfaces.**

[24]   **Smooth until all edges and mends, as well as materials, are blended in with the body of the article.**

[25]   **Set aside to dry for 24 to 36 hours.**

[26]   **Decorate with oil paints and glaze.**

[27]   **Finish glazing with New Gloss Glaze.**

damage number 11:
hairline cracks and
fractures; glass

Use System 2 for clear glass and System 1 or 3 on opaque articles.

statement of the problem

Get ready to boil your cracked article. First, examine the edges. Are the edges of the crack tight together or can you insert a razor blade between them? Is the crack dirty, or are the edges aged and yellowed or discolored? Determine whether the edges are tight together or loose, boil out any possible discoloration and dirt. Use an enamel pan or bucket big-enough and deep-enough to enable you to submerge the article. The cracked part must be completely covered. After the crack is truly clean and seems to have disappeared, air dry it, and treat the crack as follows.

step-by-step sequence

[1]   Determine whether the crack is tight or loose, that is, whether edges can be spread apart or are immovable.

[2]   Boil article; completely immerse the cracks; use a safe bleach.

[3]   Reinspect, and continue to boil until truly clean with all discoloration gone.

[4]   A few minutes before end of boiling, prepare proper cement mix for mending, repairing, or restoring. Consult the Ready Reference Chart on page 201.

[5]   Air dry.

[6]   While warm, insert a knife blade or razor's edge into the open end of the crack to open it wider. Wiggle the blade in. Do not press or force it in.

[7]   Now press cement into the crack. Use a wooden spatula (a tongue depressor will do).

[8]   Smooth paste evenly, and clean off excess; press in the cement.

[9]   Feather-out the edges until all surplus is removed and the filling is even with the adjoining surfaces.

[10]   Dry for several hours.

[11]   When dry, decorate or glaze.

If the crack is mere surface damage:

[1]   Boil as previously instructed, until invisible.

[2]   Air dry.

[3]   Apply New Gloss Glaze (boilproof) with a suitable artist brush in easy stages.

[4]   Overlay with succeeding coats, each thicker than the previous coat until you are satisfied that the article has been restored to its original luster, brilliance, and gloss.

damage number 12:   missing parts, such as heads, hands, legs, feet, wings, leaves, flowers, fruit, and similar missing parts; glass

step-by-step sequence

[1]   Classify any additional damage (flake chip, lip or edge chip, missing part, crack, or multiple breaks, and see step sequences applicable to these types of repairs).

[2]   Clean all surfaces thoroughly. Boil to loosen all foreign substances, old glue, or mending materials.

[3]   If you have to make a mold for a missing part, heat or warm until pliable a sheet of wax, and make a mold. Or:

[4]   If you prefer using plastic molding material, mix according to directions, equal parts; let set for about 8 minutes on the area of which you are making an impression. Remove, and fill the mold with the cement mixture, System 1 or 3 applicable to the article.

[5]   Fill mold, and set aside to harden overnight.

[6]   When molded material is hard, smooth edges with carbide rubber wheel set in a handgrinder. Cement in place. Use masking tape or a wax back-up mold to hold in place while repair cement is hardening.

[7]   Apply one or two coats of glaze. Let dry. Recoat with a cement mix. Feather-out the cement until it is perfectly blended with surrounding surfaces.

[8]   Reglaze repaired area with glaze. This substance can also be feathered-out. The repair should be invisible, or almost. In any case, it will be as near to perfect as is professionally possible.

how to use system 3 with other systems for mending, repairing, and restoring pottery and stoneware

This System is composed of two solid materials, Epoxybond Putty Resin and Epoxybond Putty Hardener, which are mixed together in equal parts to form a very strong adhesive material. Since this is the case, the putty mix may be used in preference to System 1 (Porcelainate) in mending heavy-bodied articles of chinaware, as well as for all articles of pottery.

It must be mentioned, in connection with mending, that pottery differs from any other ware in the density of the clay paste with which it is made. Therefore, the materials needed to mend it must be varied to meet the porosity of the article.

Stoneware is a heavy, non-porous pottery made from moist clay hardened by heat. It may be made to look fragile and lovely (Wedgwood being among the most beautiful of such examples of ware), but stoneware or earthenware is indeed heavier, tougher, harder to break, and more durable.

However, durability may be downgraded a bit when you consider how much easier it is to chip than to break. Naturally, the closer the relation of the article to glass—that is the more glass it has in it—the easier it will be to flake off a chip.

suitability of the mending material

When viewing the damage, you may have to consider an alternative method as the most suitable for your article. However, unless otherwise indicated, System 3 may be used satisfactorily to repair such damages to pottery and stoneware as these:

damage number 1: surface flake damage to the glaze; pottery and stoneware

This is the same type of damage that occurs to china or glass—small pieces of an article are chipped off the top surface and lost. The damage does not go through to the underside of the article.

If ironstone or pottery, use System 3 as follows.

step-by-step sequence

[1]   Thoroughly clean and bleach, as necessary.

[2]   Air dry.

[3]   If surface flake damage has injured the surface below the glaze, prepare Epoxybond Putty Resin and Hardener mix of equal parts, and make a firm putty of it. Color to match the article.

[4]   Fill in the damage by pressing the putty mix down into the area with your finger or with an acrylic art brush.

[5]   Carefully smooth away excess, and clean surrounding surfaces.

[6]   Permit overnight curing time. The putty mix will harden in a few minutes, but it is best to let it cure. Leave no film.

[7]   Be sure you have cleaned all film and all excess before letting the putty mix set for cure. Once cured, apply a coating of New Gloss Glaze, System 5. If necessary, repeat until mend is invisibilized.

damage number 2:   surface flake or edge chip; pottery and stoneware

step-by-step sequence

[1]   Use electric handgrinder.

[2]   Cut a grid across the damaged area.

[3]   Clean off all residue and powder with cheesecloth rag in water.

[4]   Air dry.

[5]   Prepare Epoxybond Putty Resin and Epoxybond Putty Hardener, making a fairly firm paste. Color if desirable.

[6]   Fill chip or flake.

[7]   Use art brush to press into all crevices.

[8]   Dampen fingers in water, and smooth away excess. Reduces need for sanding.

[9]   If damaged area is deep, apply two or three thin layers.

[10]   Balance in sandbox, and allow to dry between applications.

[11]   Sand gently until even with surrounding surface.

[12]   Match and mix final shade of color with New Gloss Glaze.

[13]   Apply with brush.

[14]   Feather-out until the matching repair is invisibilized.

[15]   If color matches surrounding area perfectly, apply final coat of New Gloss Glaze.

damage number 3: broken out edge chip or lip chip; pottery and stoneware

This is damage that occurs when one or two pieces in the shape of a "V" or wedge are broken in the side or lip edge of an article, and the back-up support of masking tape is required.

step-by-step sequence

[1]   Use a handgrinder to cut a grid and even the edges in a "V" shape where the chip is broken out of the edge.

[2]   Apply masking tape across the underside of open "V" area. Reinforce with Mortite or Plasticine to hold tape firm as it may sag when filler is laid in on it.

Follow Steps 3 through 15 in immediately preceding instructions.

damage number 4: broken out piece; pottery and stoneware

Chips and pieces broken off plates and similar articles, also pieces broken off handles, spouts, the bottoms of cups, and other articles.

step-by-step sequence

[1]   Study the section or piece which needs to be restored. Making the missing piece is only part of the problem. You are going to have to figure out how to anchor it once you have made it.

[2]   First, use the following method if the piece to be restored has an irregular or jagged edge:

[3]   Turn the article around and select an opposite section or piece which corresponds with the missing piece in shape and design.

[4]   Apply molding rubber. Cover both sides of an area larger than the missing piece, so that the mold will have two sides, and the hollow will be a duplicate of the missing section or piece.

[5] Plastic rubber mold will set in a few minutes. Follow directions given by the manufacturer.

[6] If you are using wax, dip the sheets of it in scalding hot water, and quickly mold it around the area of which you are making a model. As it cools, it will harden.

[7] Remove mold carefully.

[8] Trim excess by fittings. Try it over the missing section until you just about have the size for exact duplication.

[9] Mix just enough Epoxybond Putty Resin and Epoxybond Putty Hardener in equal parts to fill the mold.

[10] Put it aside to set.

[11] When the putty has hardened, remove, and discard the mold.

[12] Use handgrinder to groove out corresponding channels in edges to be unified.

[13] Fit the piece in until a snug fit is obtained.

[14] Mix a fresh batch of putty, and cement piece into place by filling the channels or grooves.

[15] Dampen your fingers with water, and smooth away excess.

[16] Apply tape to both sides of area if necessary, and set aside to harden.

[17] When hard, complete your painting and coloring to match surrounding area.

[18] Glaze.

alternate step-by-step sequence
(for missing piece with no irregularity)

[1] Place a slab of soft wax under the broken area extending it beyond break on all sides.

[2] Fold corners of wax up over edges away from missing area in order to secure wax trough. Let cool.

[3] Secure with masking tape if necessary.

[4] You now have a base on which to build the filler.

[5] Make a firm paste of Epoxybond Putty Resin and Epoxybond Putty Hardener.

[6] Smooth into area. Feather-out edges to exactly match and restore missing piece.

[7]   Dampen fingers in water, and smooth away excess.

[8]   Set aside in sandbox to harden.

[9]   When hard, use soft rubber polishing wheel to polish off any unevenness, or sand down even with all edges. Use the fingernail
test.

[10]   Decorate and glaze.

damage number 5:   an article broken in two or more pieces, such as a lamp or similar article; pottery or stoneware

A lamp must be completely dismantled—everything removed
from the pottery or stoneware body of the lamp—before repairing is undertaken.

step-by-step sequence

[1]   Inspect the surface damages to the lamp to see if there are additional spider line cracks and chips. These damages must also be
repaired in accordance with procedures set forth under their
respective headings in this chapter.

[2]   If a leaf or flower has been broken off, refer to the procedures
given under Damage Number 12. However, if the surface damage
is small and a part of the decoration, prepare cement mix in equal
parts, and apply one layer at a time, permitting time for each
layer to harden between applications, until entire damage has
been carefully concealed and the cement is even with all surrounding surfaces.

[3]   Remove any roughness or excess by lightly sanding with extremely fine sandpaper.

[4]   Prepare System 4, and blend color in to match existing walls of
the lamp.

[5]   Permit this mix to begin to set up, then apply quickly and lightly
by keeping your fingers dipped and dampened with alcohol (you
will need to apply this mix with your fingers), and by using a
feathering-out motion, match to surrounding areas.

[6]   Permit the cement to harden, and fill in any design. Permit painting to dry.

[7]   Apply final coat of New Gloss Glaze, System 5.

damage number 6:   a broken
base; pottery or stoneware

*HOW TO RESTORE A STONE-
WARE STEIN WITH A LARGE
CHIP MISSING OUT OF THE
BASE: Step 1—The missing chip pre-
sents a problem of whether to use a
handgrinder to make a grid footing in
which to anchor the mending material.
To do so would involve technical problems. Let's do it the simple way.
Working time is approximately 15 to
20 minutes. Curing time is overnight.*

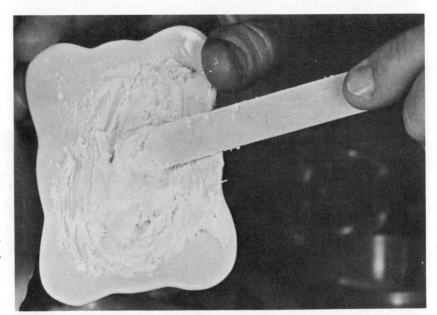

Step 2—Make a 50/50 mix of Porcelainate Powder and Hardener. Add color to match the hue of the article being mended.

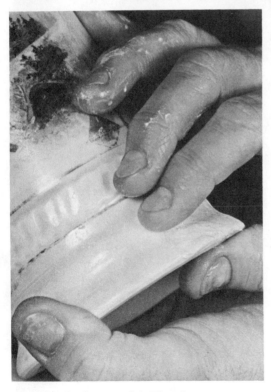

Step 3—Apply material. Thumb-press; smooth out roughness with fingers dipped in water. Use water very sparingly.

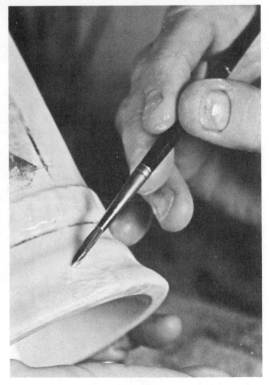

Step 4—Use brush to blend material to surrounding areas. Resmooth with outward sweep of dampened fingertips (feathering out).

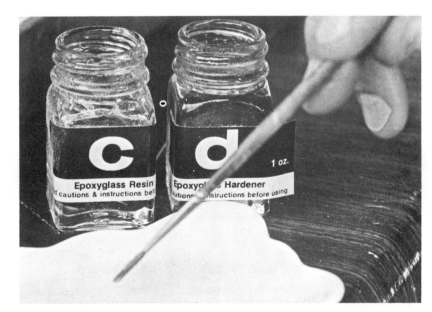

Step 5—Finishing. Porcelainize by mixing Epoxyglass Resin and Hardener with Epoxybond White Finishing Paste (System 4). Glaze if desired with New Gloss Glaze (System 5).

step-by-step sequence

[1]   Use handgrinder to make anchor grooves.

[2]   To make a mold for a missing part in a pottery or stoneware article, heat sheet wax, and make a mold.

[3]   Clean the surface of the damaged pieces.

[4]   Apply mold material. If you use plastic mold, mixture should be made of equal parts.

[5]   Apply plastic mix with a spatula. Allow setting time of 8 minutes.

[6]   Prepare a 50/50 mix of Porcelainate powder and Hardener, or you may use Epoxybond Putty Resin and Epoxybond Putty Hardener mix. Fill the mold with mixture. Permit to harden.

[7]   Remove molded piece when hard, and cement into place with additional epoxy mixture.

[8]   The repaired area can be glazed with a coat of New Gloss Glaze. When it is dry, additional thinned-out coats of epoxy mix may be added with a feathering-out motion. The mix may be thinned to a slurry by adding water or lacquer thinner.

[9]   Dampen your fingers in solvent and then in the slurry of epoxy mix to perfect this feathering-out technique.

damage number 7: a lid with a broken finial; pottery and stoneware

If a new finial is needed, follow directions given on page 43, using System 3 to restore a missing piece to pottery or stoneware.

step-by-step sequence

[1]   Prepare strips of masking tape in lengths needed to secure the piece or pieces to be fitted into the article.

[2]   Prepare Epoxybond Putty Resin and Epoxybond Putty Hardener mix in equal parts.

[3]   Cement finial into place on the lid, and secure with strips of masking tape. Set aside to dry and harden.

[4]   Examine for uneven edges and displacement. The thickness of the material you use will determine the amount of displacement. If the pieces do not fit together perfectly, wait until cement has hardened, and polish off unevenness before removing masking tape.

[5]   After polishing away ragged edges, reexamine for chips.

[6]   Remove tapes.

[7]   If you have chips, use a thick mix of Epoxybond Putty Resin and Epoxybond Putty Hardener to fill the chips in, one layer at a time, removing excess.

[8]   Place in sandbox to dry and harden.

[9]   The Epoxybond Putty Resin and Epoxybond Putty Hardener mix should be thick. Apply it with the fingers, pushing the material into the breaks of the nubs of the article and into the finial.

[10]   Now remove excess cement. If you need more, you can apply it evenly all around the mend, using your fingers dipped or dampened in water.

[11]   Clean off excess. This is extremely important, because this epoxy mix will harden into a stone-like substance, and once married to the article, is almost impossible to remove without damage to the appearance of the mend.

[12]   Remove any rough edges by adding a thin coat of the epoxy mix in a feathering-out motion. Reblend with surrounding areas.

[13]   Rebalance in sandbox, and allow to set and harden (approximately 24 hours.)

[14]   When epoxy cement is dry and hard, remove with razor blade or

grinding stone any excess film left by the cement on surrounding surfaces. The film will come off, but thick, hard epoxy cement will be virtually impossible to remove or polish without spoiling the appearance. Keep your work to a fine finish at each stage as you go.

[15] Now cream the remainder of the adhesive putty until it can be applied with a soft art brush.

[16] Apply creamy putty to the mended area, and blend it to a smooth join with surrounding surfaces.

[17] Clean off excess. This is extremely important, because this mix will harden into a stone-like substance. It is almost impossible to remove without use of the handgrinder.

[18] Remove any rough edges, and in a feathering-out motion, reblend mix with surrounding areas.

[19] Rebalance in sandbox; let set and harden approximately 24 hours.

[20] When mix is dry and hard, remove any excess. You can get film off with a razor blade. Thick, hard stone will be virtually impossible to remove. There are ways, of course; you can use a hard rubber polishing disc in a handgrinder. Do not use sandpaper; it is apt to scratch the surrounding surfaces and do additional glaze damage.

[21] Prepare epoxy mix and blend in oil color to match neighboring surfaces.

damage number 8:   a hole in the side of a vase; pottery or stoneware

step-by-step sequence

[1] If the vase is large enough for your hand to be inserted inside, apply masking tape over the hole from the inside.

[2] Surround the outside area with soft wax to the depth needed, and fill the hole, being sure to keep the article placed in the sandbox so that the area being mended is right-side up.

[3] If the vase is too small for you to work with your fingers from the inside, you can use the wooden handle of a brush or the handle of an ordinary kitchen bottle cleaner.

[4] Attach the tape very lightly to the end of the handle and ease it into the vase, smoothing it against the sides of the broken-out area.

[5]   Anchor the tape well beyond the hole, beginning at the bottom.

[6]   Use another layer of back-up tape if needed.

[7]   Fill the hole with Epoxybond Putty Resin and Epoxybond Putty Hardener mix, and leave the article balanced in the sandbox.

[8]   Allow from 24 to 36 hours for drying and curing.

[9]   As a precaution, use masking tape over the filled hole. Use tape to support and hold material in place while hardening.

[10]   When dry and hard (24 to 36 hours), remove tapes, and smooth surfaces with razor blade or handgrinder.

[11]   Apply one or two coats of mix thinned to a slurry.

[12]   If the pottery or stoneware is colored, add color to the mix material prior to filling the hole, and match the material to the article by matching exact shade in daylight.

[13]   Coat surrounding surfaces of mended article by perfectly matching epoxy mix. Feather-out material by spreading or thinning it. Keep fingers dampened in water while stroking, spreading, and feathering-out to the finest edges.

[14]   If the article is stoneware and porcelain–like in color, texture, finish, and feel, you may porcelainize over the "finished" mend by porcelainizing, use System 4 as in Step 13.

damage number 9: a broken spout; pottery and stoneware

HOW TO MEND A COFFEEPOT SPOUT: Repair or working time is approximately 20 minutes. Step 1—Use System 3. Mix the Epoxybond Putty Resin and Hardener 50/50 in sufficient quantity to build, shape, and smooth-coat the mend.

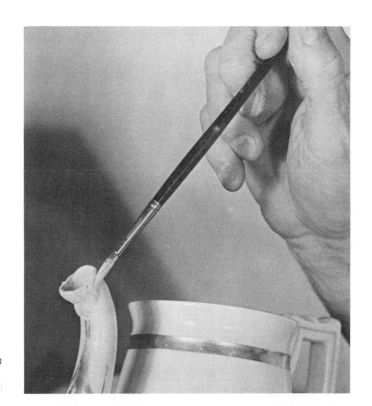

Step 2—Apply putty mix. Press into ragged edges. Smooth and shape. Let stand and harden.

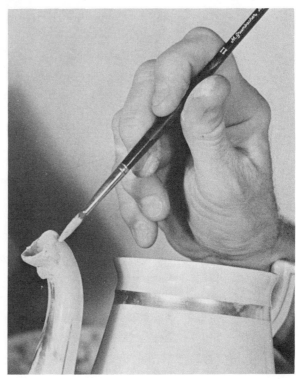

Step 3—Use System 4. Make a mix of Epoxyglass Resin and Hardener, and add Epoxybond White Finishing Paste colored to match the piece being mended.

step-by-step sequence

[1]   First, clean the pot thoroughly. Clean edges and surfaces to be restored. Boil in peroxide or washing soda to remove all stains. This will bleach out and reveal all spider cracks or other glaze damage.

[2]   Dry, and inspect damage for cracks extending from broken lip of spout down into pieces to be repaired.

[3]   Plan assembly of pieces.

[4]   Warm or oven-heat pieces to be cemented.

[5]   Prepare Epoxybond Putty Resin and Epoxybond Putty Hardener mix in equal parts.

[6]   Prepare strips of masking tape in lengths needed to secure any pieces to be cemented together.

[7]   Grind away any ragged edges.

[8]   Now, if only the end or lip of the spout is broken off, grind in anchor grooves.

[9]   Where there is a deep crack extending from the break, grind along the line of the crack, decreasing the groove as the crack grows finer.

[10] You are now ready to use putty mix to model and reshape the lip. Press clay into the line of the crack, and smooth away excess.

[11] Form a lip or pouring spout with the putty mix, and model this carefully. Maintain in place if necessary with tape. Shape it as it was, and give it a slight trough in the middle to provide good pouring.

[12] Keep smoothing and shaping the putty mix until you have restored the shape of the spout. Maintain in place with masking tape.

[13] Now, let us do a retake for a moment. If you have several pieces of broken spout, it will be necessary first to cement them together.

[14] Prepare the Epoxyglass Resin mix in equal parts.

[15] Cement all pieces together, working from the largest two down to the smallest.

[16] Tape each set to maintain adjustment of edges.

[17] Let set for 24 hours. Remove tapes.

[18] When dry, remove all excess with a razor blade (single-edge type).

[19]   Clean.

[20]   Complete cementing process until all pieces are recemented to reform the broken spout.

[21]   Balance in sandbox until dry.

[22]   Cement into place on pot, and again balance and dry in sandbox. Remove all tapes when mend is dry.

[23]   Proceed as in Steps 7 through 12.

[24]   Now for the finish. Again, prepare a mix of Epoxyglass Resin and Hardener in equal parts, and blend in oil paint to shade to match your pottery pot.

[25]   Apply with a feathering-out motion. Smooth and blend this porcelainizing material in an outward motion. Down stroke, and add covering material as needed until all signs of the mending job have disappeared completely. You may have to cover the entire spout. Be sure to go down through the open lip with an art brush and cover all signs of the hardened clay-mending material.

[26]   When satisfied that you have invisibilized the mend, set in sandbox to dry for at least 24 hours.

[27]   Decorate in accordance with motif on pot or create a new one. Use oil paints mixed with New Gloss Glaze.

[28]   Glaze with New Gloss Glaze. Use camel's-hair brush to apply. Do not use a spray glaze.

[29]   Apply gold decoration to spout as the last decorating step. If you are using art gold in the paste form, apply carefully as directed on package.

damage number 10: a broken handle; pottery and stoneware

step-by-step sequence

[1]   Study the article. Make a mold if you have to.

[2]   Use a grinder to trench out grooves in the nubs left where the handle broke off.

[3]   Grind out similar grooves in the broken pieces of the handle (if more than one piece).

[4]   Use Epoxybond Putty Resin mix to cement broken pieces together (handle only).

[5]   When handle is whole, apply to cup, or gravy boat, or tureen, or pitcher, or pot, or whatever.

[6]   Cement the two articles together by filling the grooves with the putty mix, and make sure that the edges fit together perfectly.

[7]   Use a metal clamp or tape. (A word about how to tape: Go to the inside of the article, secure the tape, bring it out over the rim, and secure it to the handle lengthwise. Fasten end to bottom of the article.

[8]   If piece is heavy and there will be too much strain on handle, re-inforce as follows: Beg some old or used drills from your dentist. Use a grinder as a drill. Drill 1/2 inch holes in the ends of the handle and through the nubs into the interior of the article.

[9]   Fill both holes in the handle with Epoxybond Putty Resin mix.

[10]   Insert end pieces of aluminum wire. (Same procedure can be used to piece broken pieces of handle together).

[11]   Let handle set and dry.

[12]   Insert wired ends of handle through holes in the nubs of the article. Bend in opposite directions until tight.

[13]   Fill holes and grooves with Epoxybond Putty Resin mix.

[14]   Tape over to secure firmly.

[15]   Also tape from inside, and bring out over handle lengthwise. Secure end of tape to bottom of article.

[16]   Allow to set.

[17]   When hard, remove tapes, and prepare for next step by smoothing away any excess. Use grinder and hard rubber polishing wheel.

[18]   Prepare equal parts of Epoxyglass Resin and Hardener with Epoxybond Resin (White Finishing Paste). Add color until the entire mix is the exact shade required to match your article.

[19]   Apply this mix with an art brush until all edges and surfaces are perfectly blended, both on the inside as well as on the outside of your mends. Use this mix to cover over the clay and wire on the inside. This mix will harden into a porcelain-like substance that matches your article. And, of course, it is unaffected by washing.

[20]   Feather-out this mix wherever applied until you have a perfect blend.

[21]   Set aside to dry in sandbox.

[22]   Glaze and decorate.

[23]   After glazing, apply art gold decoration if required.

[24]   Air dry, and reglaze if you have not used gold decoration. (The glaze will turn gold black). So, gold, *last* always.

damage number 11:   hairline cracks; pottery and stoneware

statement of the problem

Getting ready to boil your cracked article: First, examine the edges. Are the edges of the crack tight together or can you insert a razor blade between them? Is the crack dirty, or are the edges aged and yellowed or discolored? Whether the edges are tight together or loose, boil out any possible discoloration and dirt, using a safe bleaching agent. Use an enamel pan or bucket big enough and deep enough to enable you to submerge the article. The cracked part must be completely covered. After the crack is truly clean and seems to have disappeared, air dry it and treat the crack as follows:

step-by-step sequences, in general

[1]   Determine whether the crack is tight or loose; that is, whether edges can be spread apart or are immovable.

[2]   Boil article; completely immerse the cracks.

[3]   Reinspect, and continue to boil until truly clean with all discoloration gone.

[4]   A few minutes before end of boiling, prepare equal parts of Porcelainate and Hardener into paste.

[5]   Air dry.

[6]   While warm, insert a knife blade or razor's edge into the open end of the crack to open it wider. Wiggle the blade in. Do not press or force it in.

[7]   Now press cement paste into the crack. Use a wooden spatula (a tongue depressor will do).

[8]   Smooth paste evenly, and clean off excess; press in the cement. Moisten your fingers as you work to press in the cement.

[9]   Feather-out the edges until all surplus is removed and the filling is even with the adjoining surfaces.

[10]   **Dry for several hours.**

[11]   **When dry, decorate or glaze.**

Now we have a few ifs:

If the article is porcelain and *not* more than 1/16 inch thick, and *if* the crack is tight, you have repaired the crack by the above steps.

If the article is porcelain and *more* than 1/16 inch in thickness, you will have to use a handgrinder to make an "X" at the opening of the crack: On the underside, if a plate; on the inside surface, if a cup. In any case, make the "X" where least observable and where you *know* you are going to have to decorate or porcelainize over it. This is not difficult, it is just another step.

If the crack is mere surface damage or the entire surface is crazed:

1.   Boil or soak until invisible.

2.   Air dry.

3.   Apply New Gloss Glaze (boilproof) with a suitable artist brush in easy stages.

4.   Overlay with succeeding coats, each thicker than the previous coat, until you are satisfied that the article has been restored to its original luster, brilliance, and gloss.

Porcelainizing Over Your Repair:

1.   Mix Porcelainate Powder and Hardener into a paste of equal parts. (This makes a water-base paste mix).

2.   Smooth away excess.

3.   Decorate or glaze as needed. Or:
   1.   Allow porcelain filler to dry stone-hard.
   2.   Mix Epoxyglass Resin and Epoxyglass Hardener in equal parts.
   3.   Mix shade desired using oil paint (from Grumbacher oil paints).
   4.   When shade exactly matches your article, mix oil paint batch into batch of epoxy.
   5.   Apply with an art brush.
   6.   Smooth away excess until you get a perfect match with other surfaces of your article.

damage number 12: missing parts, such as heads, hands, legs, feet, fingers, wings, leaves, flowers, fruit, stems, and similar missing parts; pottery and stoneware

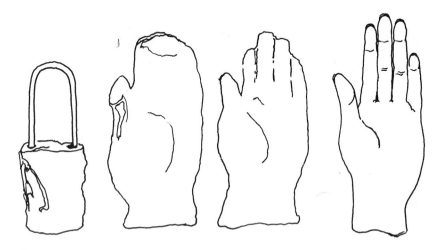

To build a hand, use baling wire fastened in a loop in a clay base form made of putty and hardener. Model the missing hand in a free-hand style in the stages shown. No previous training is needed; a hand can be built in approximately 30 minutes by an inexperienced person.

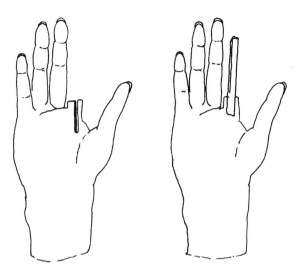

This drawing shows the mender how to make a groove at the base of a finger and insert a piece of a toothpick as a "core" in the groove, on which to rebuild the finger with putty.

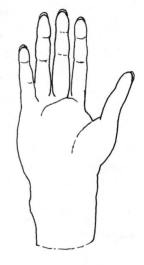

As in the previous drawing, all fingers including the thumb may be rebuilt by making a groove at the base of each missing finger, inserting a core, cementing the core firmly into the groove, permitting the cement to harden, and then proceeding to rebuild each finger with putty. Fingernail indentures are made when the putty is almost dry and about ready to set up. A hand may thus be recreated in about 1½ hours.

The drawing at the right shows joint indentures. These may be put in as the putty is about to set up.

This drawing shows joint and fingernail indentures. These are put in as the putty is about to set up. The fingers may be slightly bent to desired life-likeness. Use care. Porcelainize and color tint in flesh tones to match the rest of the figure.

*HOW TO RESTORE MISSING FINGERS ON A
PORCELAIN FIGURINE: Step 1—Examine the broken
or missing fingers.*

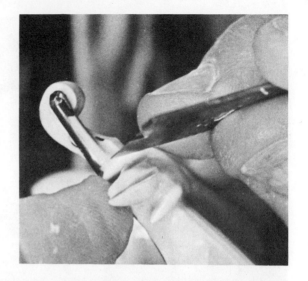

Step 2—Make a 50/50 mix of Epoxybond Putty Resin and Hardener, and press amount needed as a core into the gap. Continue to press and flatten until the putty feels smoothed to the palm and back of the china hand. Let core start to set up (about 1 hour). Use a nail file, razor blade, or small sharp knife point dampened in water or lacquer thinner (nail polish remover will do) and shape fingers as shown. Although the job appears difficult and technical, it is quite simple. You can do it!

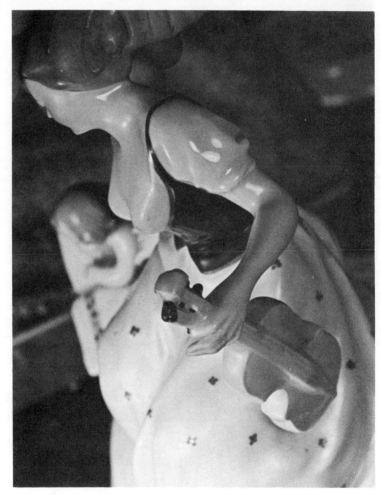

Step 3—Examine fingers from every angle to assure proper shaping all around. Consider knuckles and fingernails part of the job. Knuckles can be "bent" in while the material is still pliable. Fingernails can be pressed in with a toothpick or the point of the blade you use, whichever is easier.

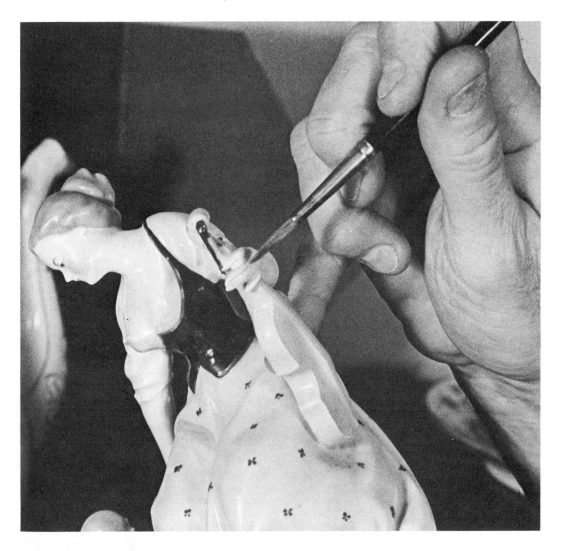

*Step 4—To finish the fingers, mix Epoxyglass Resin and
Hardener plus a bit of Epoxybond White Finishing Paste
(System 4) and add pink color to obtain flesh color
matching the figurine. Wait about 5 minutes until
material is beginning to thicken and "thread." Apply
this porcelainizing mix with an acrylic watercolor
brush or with your fingers dampened in acetone (nail
polish remover) to keep the mix from sticking to your
fingers. Smooth on and remove excess material from
between the china fingers. Glaze if desired.*

restoring hands and feet

Make a mold from a model or another figure. Obviously, you cannot make a mold of a left hand and expect it to serve as a right

hand. Usually discrepancies in size and shape can be modeled while the cast of cement from the model is drying. The part you need to make is built up roughly on a wire or on a stump with a wire loop secured in the stump. Really, much depends on your creative ability and skill. Model arms and outstretched hand with curved fingers from porcelain or clay figures free-form style without stumps or underform. Use the Epoxybond Putty Resin and Hardener to make a mix firm enough to model. Start with a small, rough model of what you want the hand, arm, finger, or whatever, to look like. Carve and model until you have a simulation of the missing part. Let this smaller-than-needed model harden and when hard, build it up with additional, wet, creamy cement mix, until you have the form needed. Let that harden, and cement it in place. Porcelainizing and coloring come as a last step.

step-by-step sequence

[1]   **Anchor the molded piece where there is a projection, nub, or stump into which you can grind a groove or footer.**

[2]   **If there is no nub, use a small amount of System 3, and create the stump required. Allow the projection to set and harden. It can be shaped and grooved later when stone-hard.**

[3]   **When hard, grind the footer through the center of the nub. Use a fine cutting wheel on a handgrinder.**

[4]   **Keep the "cut" light—not deep—so as not to chip or weaken the projection.**

[5]   **Carefully insert a fine, flat stick, such as the fine end of a toothpick. The length should be in proportion to the length of the finger you are making.**

[6]   **If you are making an arm, you should use a bent piece of pewter wire. Pewter is not springy. Hardware stores sell it under the name of soldering wire. This kind of wire can be twisted and bent to the contour required, and it will stay that way.**

[7]   **This same wire can be flattened at one end, delicately bent, and inserted in the channel you make for a finger. It can serve equally well as the skeleton structure on which to mold a leg or foot. Other examples of use include a shepherd's staff, a cane, and like articles.**

making a hand (the core) and fingers

Sizes of hands vary. Details of the position of the fingers vary. The characteristics of male and female hands reveal considerable difference in size, thickness, and expression. These differences extend to a variety of difficulties in copying, creating or mending, repairing, and restoring.

If a hand or arm is missing, careful measurements of the remaining hand must be made. If both hands and arms are missing, measure straight down from your own shoulder to a point midway between hip and knee. This measurement will give you an overall length of arm and hand. Thus, you might have a ratio of 14 inches to 12 inches to 9 inches. These numbers could serve as a scale in eights of an inch, sixteenths, or thirty-seconds of an inch. You will observe your upper arm is slightly longer than your forearm. And, again, the core of your hand (palm span) is usually somewhat longer than the fingers extending from it.

To get the feel of what you are doing, place your own hand on a piece of paper, fingers close together, and draw an outline of your hand. Measure across from the outside of your thumb knuckle (at the outside point of the knuckle) to the widest spread point of flesh below your smallest finger. This will give you hand-width measurement. Also, measure the length measurement from the base of your middle finger to the wrist line. These proportions will guide you in making a stump or core of the hand you are required to make or create, in miniature as well as in life-size.

step-by-step sequence

[1] Build the core with System 3, Epoxybond Putty Resin mix.

[2] Cut grooves needed in the arm stump, as shown in the illustration, while the putty is beginning to set up.

[3] Flatten the end of the wire, and cut off to the length required to make a loop. When the putty mix feels like it is getting firm, insert the ends of the wire loop, and permit the putty to harden.

[4] Build the hand-core of putty mix over and around the looped wire until it is completely concealed. This wire frame will firmly hold the putty and help you form the core required. Let it set.

[5] Shape and contour as shown in the second illustration.

[6] Cut in the anchor grooves.

[7] Shape the palm, and begin to contour the palm-span and outline of the main part of the hand. Use a handgrinder. Correct mistakes by adding putty mix and permitting it to set and harden.

[8] Place the fingers you have prepared (of wire bent to shape desired) and anchor each one in the prior-prepared groove you have cut into the core of the hand. Position each finger properly and correctly, as you will not be able to do so later.

[9]   Apply putty mix around the base of each finger, and permit this to set, thus firmly anchoring each finger.

[10]   Build each finger of putty mix. Shape and contour with an art brush (stiff acrylic type) and dip it into solvent as needed. Each finger will need shaping and contouring. Permit putty mix to set up; just before it hardens, press in the indentation needed on each finger tip to resemble a fingernail.

[11]   If the putty has hardened or the finger is too delicate to do the pressing needed, add just a wee bit more of the putty mix with a slurry consistency, and barely touch the fingertip with the amount needed. This may best be done with a fine brush of camel's-hair or sable. (Be sure to clean the brush after such a use.)

[12]   Wait a few minutes until setting-up begins, and make indentation or nail mark with the end of a toothpick.

[13]   Reexamine after the finger has hardened for size, shape, positioning, contour, and eye-rightness.

[14]   Prepare a slurry of System 3 to resurface the entire hand and fingers as necessary, and to smooth, even-up the joins, reshape here and there, retouch, recontour, and cover up any roughness of surface or outline. Use an extremely thin slurry for this work. Also a fine sable art brush consisting of just the fewest possible number of hairs in it, well-pointed, is recommended.

[15]   Permit resetting when eye-rightness has been achieved.

[16]   Porcelainize, tint to natural shade, and glaze.

other damage to hands, fingers, arms, and legs

step-by-step sequence

[1]   Inspect damaged figure for broken hands, arms and legs, and also for cracks and chips. These will have to be repaired in accordance with procedures for same given under their respective headings in this chapter.

[2]   If your article has a broken hand and is chipped, cracked and broken in more than three pieces, it may not be worth your time and the good materials it will take to restore it. A careful inspection will help you decide.

[3]   Plan assembly of the broken pieces.

[4]   Prepare strips of tape for the broken pieces.

[5]   Prepare clay cement mix in equal parts.

[6]   Cement pieces into place in the article, secure with strips of masking tape from both the inside and the outside, and set aside to dry and harden.

[7]   Examine for uneven edges and displacement. The thickness of the material you use will determine the amount of displacement. If the pieces do not fit together perfectly, wait until cement has hardened, and grind off unevenness before removing masking tape.

[8]   After grinding away ragged edges, reexamine for chips.

[9]   Remove tapes.

[10]   If you have chips, you should use the Epoxybond Putty Resin to fill them in, removing all excess.

[11]   Place in sandbox, or balance in a bed of wax, to dry and harden.

[12]   Sand smooth any remaining rough edges.

[13]   If you have to mold a missing part, see System 1.

[14]   For finishing, cream the remainder of the clay until it can be applied with a soft art brush.

[15]   Apply creamy cement to the mended area, and blend it to a smooth join with surrounding surfaces.

[16]   Clean off excess. This is extremely important, because this clay cement mix will harden into a stone-hard substance, and once married to your article, is almost impossible to remove.

[17]   Remove rough edges with solvent, and in a feathering-out motion, reblend cement with surrounding areas.

[18]   Rebalance in wax bed or sandbox, and let set and harden approximately 24 hours.

[19]   When cement is dry and hardened, remove with a razor blade or very fine sandpaper any excess film left by cement on surrounding surfaces. You can get film off. Thick, hard cement will be virtually impossible to remove. There are ways, of course; you can use a hard rubber polishing wheel in a handgrinder. Sandpaper, if not used carefully, is apt to scratch surrounding surfaces and do additional glaze damage.

[20]   Prepare epoxy porcelainizing mix, and blend in oil color to match article. Porcelainize mended surfaces.

[21]   Smooth until all edges and mends, as well as materials, are blended in with the body of the article.

[22]   Set aside to dry for 24 to 36 hours.

[23]   **Decorate with oil paints and New Gloss Glaze.**

[24]   **Finish glazing with New Gloss Glaze.**

small missing parts

Usually, a small missing part such as a nose, ear, finger, shoe buckle, or toe, requires nothing more than a dab of cement mix, to approximate the size and shape as needed. Finish downward as the mix begins to set. Do not let the part get hard, because you can get a nicer shape by using a stiff art brush dipped in solvent. Use a toothpick to poke indentations for nostrils in a nose. The end of this same little toothpick can be used to make fingernail indentations on fingers. Always put such details in before porcelainizing or finishing.

how to use system 4 with other systems for high-gloss finishing (porcelainizing) for pottery

This System is composed of the two compounds in System 2, Epoxyglass Resin and Epoxyglass Hardener, with the addition of Epoxybond Resin (White Finishing Paste), which can be added to the mixture as it is needed. Color can also be added as required. This System is used to give a high-gloss finish to any mended article except that of clear glass. It can be applied with a brush after the mending, and used to decorate an article after it has been completed, including one of colored glass. The one exception to this rule is the use of gold pastes, gold powder, or gold leaf, all of which must be added after the finishing material. The use of this System to achieve gold or silver leaf, and copper, pink, or silver luster effects is given in Chapter 6 under decorative finishes.

how to use system 5, new gloss glaze, with other systems for restoring pottery

This is a liquid which can be used with a brush directly from the bottle for glazing all mended articles. It contains volatile solvents that should be kept away from heat, sparks, and open flame, and used with adequate ventilation. When not in use, the container should be kept tightly closed, as with all liquid mending materials. It is used to repair glaze damage to chinaware, pottery, and stoneware as follows:

1.   Start with clear New Gloss Glaze (boilproof).*
2.   Thin with lacquer thinner or glaze thinner.
3.   Brush gently on damaged area.
4.   Air dry.
5.   Apply several more coats until even with surrounding edges of undamaged glazed surface.
6.   Feather-out slightly as you brush on last coat.

how to clean articles that have been previously mended

Articles of china, glass, and pottery that have been previously mended require complete cleaning before the miracle-mending systems are used to repair and restore them.

Cleaning can be accomplished by several means. The article may be placed in an enamel bucket or other container large enough to submerge all the broken areas, and soaked in Clorox. When the old mending material has been loosened and the pieces come apart, they should be wiped, scraped, thoroughly cleaned, and dried. The Clorox will not in any way damage the article or its decoration. It should be used according to directions for any household purposes.

Another method of cleaning is to boil the article, again using an enamel container, in a strong solution of washing soda or industrial peroxide. Both the soaking and boiling operations can be repeated as often as necessary to accomplish complete cleaning.

In cleaning such glass articles as decanters and perfume bottles that have lime deposits inside (a condition that is called "sick glass"), steam-iron cleaners, which are readily available and safe, should be tried. If the bottles are very old and the lime deposits considerable, hydrofluoric acid may be used. This is

---

*Color may be added, but must be done in very good light to obtain a perfect match.

obtainable from industrial chemists or a wholesale chemical supply house. It should be used with extreme caution, because it can give a dangerous burn. When used on poor-quality glass, it will produce a slight haze or iridescent frost on the interior unless rinsed out almost immediately with cold water.

The use of miracle-mending materials described in this book and used according to the step-by-step procedures outlined, together with the increasing skill and experience of a mender, will generally produce miracle results. Some mending can be invisibilized and the mended article restored to normal use. Occasionally, however, a mender discovers that the materials and techniques that have produced perfect results time and again on articles of china, glass, and pottery may *not* produce the same results with other articles that appear to be similar.

The cause of this problem may be in the composition, age, or source of the article. A wide variety of materials from the earth are used in a variety of combinations in making different kinds of articles of china, glass, and pottery. For example, glass may contain lead, lime, or silver, and some of the compounds in glassware may be nonresponsive to mending materials, while apparently similar articles may be easily and perfectly mended.

Occasionally, there *is* an element of chance that must be taken into account in mending. The flaw or fault may be inherent in the composition of the article itself, rather than in the mending materials or the careful skill of the mender.

miracle-mending materials applied to china

The miracle-mending materials, properly used, enable you to mend almost any damaged or broken article made of china. The mending materials, as you have learned, are complex chemical compounds of the laboratory. Chinaware is made in and comes from the Orient, Continental Europe and England, and America.

Chinaware is made from a combination of earth substances, with which the miracle-mending materials have been designed to have a special affinity, that is, a special bonding capability. The understanding by the mender of this fact, with the use of the proper materials to mend each type of broken chinaware, makes the miracle of perfect mending come true.

China, which is the product to be covered in this chapter, is the name given to a wide variety of articles that may be referred to elsewhere herein as Oriental Export, Continental European, English, and American (see Appendix). Chinaware may be useful and beautiful, commonplace and rare, easily replaced or duplicated, or treasures lost forever to collectors and museums, if not valued enough to preserve, mend, repair, or restore.

chinaware

The name comes from China where the product was first made many centuries ago—perhaps as early as 206 B.C. to 220 A.D.—definitely a flourishing business by the ninth and tenth centuries. Chinaware is characteristic of a cultural heritage and a love of beauty that is centuries older than that of European countries.

what chinaware
is made of

From the beginning, chinaware was made of two earth substances, petuntse and kaolin, made by crushing granite rock (felsite) until, with the addition of water, the mass attains the consistency of clay. The basic difference between the two is that quartz, which forms a considerable part of petuntse, is not present in kaolin. When these two clays are mixed, they reinforce each other. The kaolin makes the mixture more easily molded and modeled. Because of its quartz content, petuntse fuses with the mixture completely to form the hard, glassy, translucent surface that is characteristic of "true" porcelain. If broken, the break in the porcelain article will show striation which has a grained appearance that looks moist and lucid, like glass, and resembles that of polished wood. This type of chinaware is known as *hard paste* porcelain. It is brilliantly white, cold to the touch, impervious to liquids and even to scratching. The resin of mending System 3 is the equivalent of kaolin, and the Porcelainate of System 1 has its appearance.

varieties of chinaware

oriental export
(chinaware)

Hard paste porcelain was made in China and Japan. In China, the making of porcelain centered in the community of Chingtechen where, by the thirteenth century, the entire population was engaged in some way in the porcelain-making process. The Japanese began to make porcelain about 1500. It is called Imari, after the port from which most of the products were shipped. The body of Japanese porcelain is inferior in quality to that of Chinese, but the decoration is much richer and more diverse.

Although not unknown in the courts of Europe, Oriental Export chinaware was introduced by the great trading companies in Europe during the eighteenth century. It was greatly admired and highly prized. The name *porcelain* was given to it in Europe because of the resemblance of the finish to a lovely, colorful, glossy tropical marine shell found in the Mediterranean area.

The term *Oriental Export Porcelain* is used to describe all pieces *made* and *decorated* in the Orient more or less according to

Western specifications and for Western use, that is, for export only. The trade in this material was developed into a significant phase of international commerce during the eighteenth century, carried on principally between China and Europe. Prior to the American Revolution, English trade laws, for tax purposes, prohibited the importing of any Oriental commodities—even tea— except through England. The direct importing of chinaware into the United States began in 1784, and was never extensive.

Chinaware exported from the Orient falls into two general classes: The ordinary varieties, which were either left undecorated or painted in underglazed colors of which blue-and-white was most popular; and porcelain made to special order. The latter includes armorial porcelain with decorations painted over the glaze, such as the 302-piece table service, with the arms of the Society of Cincinnati, purchased by George Washington in 1786 for use at Mount Vernon (Martha Washington's "company china"). The latter also includes porcelain with "personalized" coats-of-arms or other family identification.

Oriental Export chinaware, unlike most porcelains, has no factory or other marks on the back. Any piece of so-called Oriental Export which has a mark, especially a square pseudo-Chinese mark in red with a running "S" beside it, was made in France. It is an imitation known as Samson, the name of the French manufacturer, who also imitated Meissen, Chelsea, and Bow chinaware.

All Oriental Export chinaware is 150 or more years old. For this reason, minor hairline cracks, small nicks, or minor repairs are to be expected. Elinor Gordon, an American collector, says, "Many collectors are willing to overlook small nicks, chips, or age cracks. It would be foolish to miss the opportunity of acquiring a rare piece because it is imperfect." Such opinions have inspired the creation of miracle-mending materials for the collector as well as the novice.

continental
european chinaware

Craftsmen in Europe, examining the imported chinaware, believed it was some kind of glass, and began experiments to reproduce it. They mixed ground glass, lime, soapstone, potash, and sometimes bone-ash, with white clay and other materials to produce a type of china that is known as *soft paste*. This china lacks the cold, brilliant perfection of "true" porcelain; but when glazed with oxide of lead or tin, has a beautiful finish. Like hard paste porcelain, soft paste porcelain is made of earth clays; but the soft paste china is first fired in "biscuit" or bisque stage, that is, unglazed. After the initial firing, decorating is done and a glaze of lead applied before a second firing at lower temperature. Soft paste porcelain is not nearly as resistant as hard paste to liquids or stain, and articles can be easily scratched with a nail file or knife. When broken, the break shows a grainy or sugary surface. The lead coating appears to "sit" on the surface rather than becoming a part of the article. This gives a depth and richness to the decoration, which seems to glow through as though illuminated from behind. No re-firing is necessary in mending, repairing, or restoring.

meissen and dresden chinaware

Nowhere in Europe was Oriental Export china more popular than in Germany. The rage for this porcelain and for other forms of Oriental art reached its height in the Japanese palace in Dresden, which was never completed. The palace was planned by Augustus the Strong, Elector of Saxony and King of Poland, who wanted every room decorated exclusively with porcelain of which he had thousands of pieces.

Augustus ordered a young alchemist, Johann Friedrich Bottger, to turn his talents from a search for gold by transmutation to a search for the secret of manufacturing porcelain. With the aid of a physicist and mathematician, Tschirnhausen, Bottger was able to do this in 1706, and by 1710, he had established a factory at Meissen, a suburb of Dresden. Augustus had not only the very first hard paste porcelain made in Europe (and as much of it as he wanted since he owned the factory), but all his Chinese pieces as well. Meissen, from 1710 throughout most of the eighteenth century, was produced and decorated by the leading painters of Europe and represents some of the most beautiful and treasured porcelain extant in the world.

This porcelain was known for many years by the name of the Saxon capital, Dresden; however, many other factories sprang up to make commercial china, and the term "Meissen" is now used to identify the old, royal porcelain, while "Dresden" is used for both old and modern china made in other factories. The china menders were not far behind nor long in developing techniques to restore broken treasures.

The difference between Oriental Export porcelain, or China-Trade porcelain, and that made at the royal factory at

Meissen and later in other European countries, lies in the forms and decorations used. All are hard paste porcelain, made from the same types of clay, and all can be mended with Systems 1, 2, and 4.

english chinaware

Beginning in the early 1740s, factories for making soft paste chinaware were started in England at Bow and Chelsea and Bristol, Derby, and Worcester; however, no hard paste porcelain was made until about 1768, when a Quaker named Cookworthy discovered deposits of kaolin and petuntse near Plymouth, and took out the first patent for making hard paste chinaware. Thereafter, with the formulas for both soft paste porcelain and hard paste porcelain generally available, the various manufacturers produced whatever the market demanded.

Between the years 1790 and 1810, there came into existence in England a hybrid that was to be known as English bone china. The most prominent name in connection with its development is Josiah Spode, father and son.

The Spode formula was roughly 4 parts of china stone (petuntse) to 3 1/2 parts of china clay (kaolin), with the addition of 6 parts of bone ash, a powdery white calcium phosphate ash produced by burning animal bones. When these three components are fired, the result is a hard paste porcelain softened by the addition of the bone ash. It wears better and is harder and less permeable than soft paste porcelain, but has the same soft type of glaze. It is whiter than soft paste porcelain, but less white and brilliant than hard paste porcelain. Because the new type of china, which has come to be known as English bone china, had the desirable qualities of both hard and soft paste porcelain and could be made considerably more economically, it became generally popular. Today, most of the good quality table services produced in England and the United States are bone china. Because of its powdery white base, the Porcelainate of System 1 is especially useful in its repair and restoration.

suggested approach to mending a china article

1. Determine whether the article is worth the time and the relatively small cost of mending materials. If the article can be easily and inexpensively replaced, that is one matter. If it belongs to a table service or a set or a pair, and cannot be replaced, mend it. If the article has sentimental value to you or is a piece of intrinsic value and beauty, by all means mend it. (Visiting antique shops and attending antique shows may provide some pleasant surprises about the increasing value of old china). The decision about mending is up to you.

2. Study the broken or damaged article carefully. It may be helpful, at first, for you to make a list on paper of the damages: flake, surface flake or chip, edge or lip chip, missing piece or pieces, cracks and fractures, broken off handles, spouts, finials, and knobs. Do you have them, whole or broken, or have they been lost?

3. Decide on the order in which these damages are to be repaired. How much can you do at one sitting using the same mix? Time can be saved if you have several pieces of china to be repaired (such as several plates, saucers, cups, and other pieces of a table service, with similar damages on each piece) and can work on all the pieces at one work session. Also, if several missing pieces must be made using molds, these can be made at one work session, and restored to the article at another. Remember that adequate time for drying and hardening of mending materials must be allowed.

4. Select the proper miracle-mending system for each job. At this point, consult the Ready Reference Chart on page 201.

There is a *general rule* that:

System 1 is used for repairing damages to hard paste and soft paste porcelain (chinaware), and for restoring missing pieces.

System 2 is used for mending, repairing, and restoring glass and china.

System 3 is used for mending, repairing, and restoring hard and soft paste pottery, such as stoneware, faience, and majolica.

System 4 is used for high-gloss finishing (porcelainizing) on china, colored glass, pottery, and some stoneware.

System 5 is used for all glaze damage and for glazing nearly all articles that are mended.

There are exceptions to this general rule that a mender, who wishes to become really proficient, will learn by experience to recognize. A careful study of the Ready Reference Chart, page 201, will be most helpful.

5. Determine the kind of china you plan to mend. The marks put on the bottom or back of an article by the manufacturer will help.

how to mend
a cream pitcher

For one reason or another almost everyone loves a pitcher. It can be any kind and it excites a certain amount of interest, perhaps because it is one of man's earliest artifacts, and certainly one that has always challenged the ceramist for design, elegance, beauty, and usefulness. A pitcher does the unique kind of serving job that no other serving piece accomplishes in quite the same way. In addition, it has become an article that is singled out by collectors the world over—there is no question about mending a pitcher. You and I will always want to do it if we know how. So let us begin with the problem.

statement of the problem

The problem with a pitcher is that it can have so many things go wrong with it when broken. It is a piece that always has a handle that must support the pitcher as well as the weight of what it contains. Then, there is the base that must be viewed for the pitcher's support. The sides may be bell-shaped, and the spout is almost always given a beautiful shape for pouring. Last but not least, you may have a very intricate and lovely patterned decoration or motif of fruits, flowers, or birds on the handle as well as the sides. Let me say right here, if you can repair a pitcher with all the multiple fractures, breaks, abrasions, chips, and pattern damage it can suffer when dropped, you can repair any article of chinaware, antique or modern.

So let us look over our materials and select our mending cement. You may find you need more than one kind for more than one problem situation during progress of the repair. In any case, set out all the materials and equipment you may need.

Mending, even when you have all the materials and equipment handy, is not a slow process as some may think. It takes patience and a pair of capable hands, but the work goes swiftly, changing from one procedure or step to another with rapid precision. One must not delay when cement has been mixed, because the batch soon fudges—usually 5 to 20 minutes, depending on the proportions used. So let us move right along with the step sequences on how to mend a cream pitcher.

step-by-step sequence

[1]   Inspect damaged pieces for broken spout, handle, or cracks and chips. These will have to be repaired in accordance with procedures for same given under respective headings elsewhere in this book.

[2]   If your article has a broken handle and is chipped, cracked, and broken in more than three pieces, you will have to decide on its value to you. As far as mending is concerned, it may not be worth your time and the good materials it will take to restore it. A careful inspection will help you decide.

[3]   Plan assembly of the broken pieces.

[4]   Prepare strips of masking tape in lengths needed to secure the pieces to be fitted into the article.

[5]   Prepare the cement mix (System 1 or 3).

[6]   Cement pieces into place in the article, secure with strips of masking tape from both the inside and the outside, and set aside to dry and harden.

[7]   Examine for uneven edges and displacement. The thickness of the material you use will determine the amount of displacement. If the pieces do not fit together perfectly, wait until cement has hardened, and grind off unevenness before removing masking tape.

[8]   After grinding away ragged edges, reexamine for chips.

[9]   Remove tapes.

[10]   If you have chips, you should use Porcelainate mix (System 1) to fill the chips in, removing all excess.

[11]   Place in sandbox to dry and harden.

[12]   Sand smooth any remaining rough edges.

[13]   If you have to put on a broken handle, cement the pieces together. Let harden.

[14]   Grind a grid in the top and bottom nubs on the article, and grind grooves in top and bottom of handle. You can put in a cross shape ("**X**") or a single groove.

[15]   The base cement should be firm. Press the cement into the grooves of the article's nubs and into the handle. Use System 3.

[16]   Apply tape to inside of article, and bring a long-enough piece of it out over the edge to secure the handle in place.

[17]   Now cream the remainder of the adhesive putty until it can be applied with a soft art brush.

[18]   Apply creamy cement to the mended area, and blend it to a smooth join with handle and surrounding surfaces.

[19]   Clean off excess. This is extremely important, because this clay cement mix will harden into a stone-hard substance and, once married to the article, is almost impossible to remove.

[20]   Remove any rough edges with a razor blade, and in a feathering-out motion, reblend cement with surrounding areas.

[21]   Rebalance in sandbox, and let set and harden for approximately 24 hours.

[22]   When cement is dry and hard, remove any excess film left by cement on surrounding surfaces with a razor blade. Film you can get off. Thick, hard stone will be virtually impossible to remove. There are ways, of course; you can use a hard rubber polishing disc in a handgrinder, or sandpaper. However, sandpaper is apt to scratch surrounding surfaces and do additional glaze damage.

[23]   Prepare epoxy mix, and blend in oil color to match article. Porcelainize mended surfaces.

[24]   Smooth until all edges and mends, as well as materials, are blended in the body of the article.

[25]   Set aside to dry for 24 to 36 hours.

[26]   Decorate with oil paints and New Gloss Glaze.

[27]   Finish glazing with New Gloss Glaze (System 5).

how to mend ornamental articles and decorative accessories, such as porcelain birds

HOW TO RE-STORE A BEAK ON A BOEHM PORCELAIN BIRD: Step 1— Examine where the beak has been broken off. Ordinarily notches should be ground in to provide a "footing" for the mending material. However, this method is technical and not necessary in this instance.

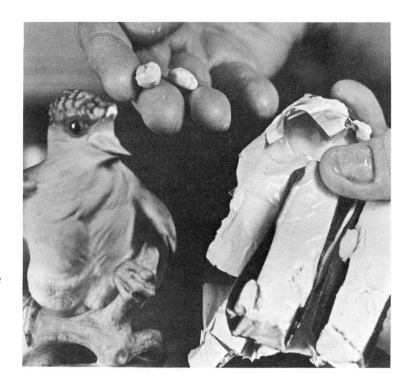

Step 2—Use Epoxybond Putty Resin and Hardener. Make the putty mix using 50/50 of the light and dark putty. Color to the hue needed to match the lower beak and blend in with the bird's topknot.

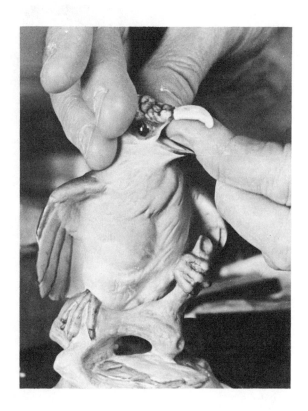

Step 3—Apply, press, and shape the putty until it begins to look like a beak.

113

Step 4—As the putty begins to set up, shape as needed, and pinch off excess material with your fingers dampened in thinner. Water will do.

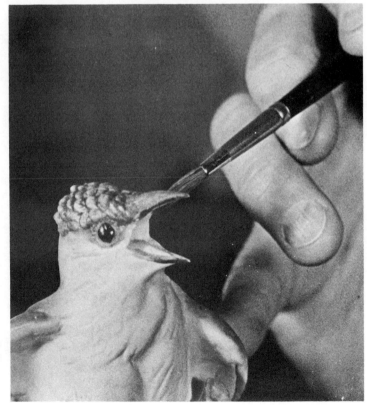

Step 5—Finishing. The beak is done with a brush, as shown, using a bit of coloring material to obtain a perfect match. When material is dry, apply a coat of New Gloss Glaze, or if the finish of the bird is matte or bisque (a dull sheen), do not glaze. The natural oil from your fingers will be sufficient to give the beak a "shine" when rubbed a little. Mending time is 15 to 20 minutes. Was it worth it? Curing time is about 2 hours.

statement of the problem

Birds are not easy to mend because of the thin porcelain with which most of them are made. Many of them have a bisque finish. Some of these birds may be rare specimens made by a great artist, such as Kandler, who worked at the Meissen factory in the early eighteenth century. There are contemporary greats too, such as Boehm and Doughty. The thinness of the porcelain and the bisque finish are only part of the problem.

There are other problems in mending birds, such as how to replace or cement an outstretched wing onto the body. Also, the wing itself can be in shards. There may be feet or claws to consider. These will be as difficult to mend or restore, if missing, as fingers on a hand. Making a mold of a missing part may not be as hard to do as getting the bird into a balanced and satisfactory position that will permit a good join.

I mention these problems as you will certainly encounter them in mending birds. And I may add, these same problems are intensified in restoration of a bird made of crystal. The question is, can you mend them if you are not professional?

In regard to being professional as contrasted with nonprofessional, the difference lies in your own personal attitude and degree of versatility and skill.

There are no materials, equipment, or procedures mentioned in this book that are not employed in professional work. How you use them to produce a professional result remains with you. Properly used they will give you excellent results. Skillfully used, these materials and step sequences will enable you to produce highly professional work and invisible mending.

One suggestion may be worthwhile to you at this point. Approach any repair in an analytical frame of mind and in a creative mood. To recreate a treasured article means more than just gluing it together. Creative ability added to technique and know-how is professional. And certainly when you are mending birds, fruits, flowers, dogs, horses, lions, and other beautiful creatures created by master ceramists and glassblowers, you will want to make a master mend.

Lacking skill or courage to attempt a "master" or professional mend, I would suggest you study the things wrong with the article—the damage, the breakage, the missing parts—and make a list on paper of what should be done to restore it. Such an analysis is generalship to say the least, and the battle is half-won, because when you see on paper what must be done, you will know what materials and equipment will be needed to do the job.

You will also realize what steps in the mending procedure you will have to take. In addition you may plan how to eliminate some of the problems.

Let us say you have a Doughty bird group; they are in flight, each one a step above the other, held in aerial suspension above the sea (the base); and let us say they are, or were, suspended, because the lowest of the three has his claws and legs extended to clutch the spar on the top mast of a ship almost completely hidden beneath the waves. This beautiful group is broken badly. What are the mending or recreative problems? Certainly the article is worth restoring. Part of two of the birds' wings are missing. The base is damaged. Some of the white foam-flecked porcelain of the curl running across the tops of the waves is damaged. But never mind that! You have saved every tiny shard. An even bigger problem is balance. How is the wing of the lowest bird going to support by contact of mere wing tips the two flying birds above? Can it be done with the materials and equipment you have? The answer is yes, of course.

To accomplish the job you will want all the available props you can lay your hands on. In addition, you may invent a few. For just such a mend, you may have to go to the nearest hickory bush and cut out pieces the shape of a slingshot or "Y" or use a Tinkertoy Erector Set *supported by gobs of plasticine.*

approach to the problem

First measure the height from the base to the highest bird. Make sure the sandbox is deep enough in sand to support the props.

Throw away the shards! You will find it better mending judgment to cement the basic pieces of an article together, and then fill in or make the missing part by modeling it in clay right onto the object as you work. Recreate the article! The clay listed as one of the materials you will work with is an adhesive. You will learn that it adheres as you model it to the article being repaired.

This clay can be "creamed" either with water or solvent. Extremely beautiful and delicate tracery work can be executed. Dip into it with a good acrylic brush and complete the design over the basic. In the example we are discussing, the shards you threw away may have been part of the bird's wing feathers. You can duplicate them freehand with this clay and your brush. If you think you do not have such talent (even though you probably do), make a wax mold. Warm your molding wax, and apply it before any of the broken pieces have been cemented into place.

You are going to need to restore each bird to its original form before you can group them together. Do all the mending you can do first on each piece. Leave the bringing-together of all units to the last, as you will have serious balance problems to overcome in this highly decorative group.

Plan to use stable props for balance. By that, I mean do not use any prop that has any give or springiness in it. For each contact, wing tip to wing tip, you must support the articles to be joined so that their point of contact is sure, firm, and immobilized. Never mind the finish—that is standard procedure given last in the step-by-step sequence.

Once the molding, remodeling, and mending of each piece is completed, you will be ready to regroup your pieces and re-create the original.

Your approach at this stage of mending may require you to cement two birds together, wing tip to wing tip. Balance them in the sandbox on their opposite wings, breasts or legs. If they cannot be immobilized in sand with "Y" props, set them in the wax bed. If this does not work, suspend one of the birds on a string from an open shelf, set the other bird in wax or sand, and bring it into contact with the suspended bird. Use your clay cement mix, as well as tape, to join their wing tips. The clay cement hardens into stone, and it is strong enough when hard to support the suspended bird.

This process may be repeated in joining the two birds to the third or lowest bird. You may have to use a similar procedure in joining the low bird to the ship spar.

Once joined and recreated as a group, you will be ready to complete restoration of any remaining defects.

step-by-step sequence

[1] Inspect broken pieces for cracks and chips.

[2] These will have to be repaired in accordance with procedures for same given in Chapter 2.

[3] Plan assembly of the broken pieces.

[4] Prepare strips of masking tape in lengths needed to secure the pieces to be fitted into the article.

[5] Prepare the cement mix in equal parts.

[6] Cement pieces into place in the article, secure with strips of masking tape from both the inside and the outside, and set aside to dry and harden.

[7]   Examine for uneven edges and displacement. The thickness of the material you use will determine the amount of displacement. If the pieces do not fit together perfectly, wait until cement has hardened, and grind off unevenness before removing masking tape.

[8]   After grinding away ragged edges, reexamine for chips.

[9]   Remove tapes.

[10]   If you have chips, you should use the Porcelainate mix to fill the chips in, removing all excess.

[11]   Cream your cement mix, using System 3.

[12]   Add additional coats to smooth over any rough edges.

[13]   Let harden 24 to 36 hours.

[14]   Now cream the remainder of the mix until it can be applied with a soft art brush.

[15]   Apply creamy cement to the mended area, and blend it to a smooth join with surrounding surfaces.

[16]   Clean off excess. This is extremely important because this cement mix will harden into stone.

[17]   Smooth and remove any rough edges, and in a feathering-out motion, reblend cement with surrounding areas. To draw in the feather designs, use a stiff, very fine point on a brush or a quill as the mix begins to set.

[18]   Rebalance in sandbox or wax, and let set and harden for approximately 24 hours.

[19]   When cement is dry and hard, gently remove any excess film left by cement on surrounding surfaces with solvent. You can get film off. Thick, hard stone will be virtually impossible to remove. There are ways, of course; you can use a hard rubber polishing disc in a handgrinder, but it will take great care and a very delicate touch. So, it is better to get the excess off first.

[20]   Prepare epoxy mix, and blend in oil color to match article. Porcelainize mended surfaces.

[21]   Smooth until all edges and mends, as well as materials, are blended in with the body of the article.

[22]   Set aside to dry for 24 to 36 hours.

[23]   Decorate with oil paints mixed with New Gloss Glaze.

[24]   Finish glazing with New Gloss Glaze (System 5).

how to mend porcelain figurines (dresden, meissen, and other german, french, and italian examples)

Shown is an example of a figure with lacework restoration created by dipping fine net material in liquid porcelain mixture, and when drying begins to set in, by draping and cementing porcelainized net material onto the figure.

Problems in mending a figurine arise in restoring hands and feet, arms and legs, lacy garments, and missing parts. These cause a lot of problems, but all can be resolved.

statement of the problem

Porcelain figures are usually small and fairly easily mended. Some of the problems mentioned above such as a shattered hand and arm or a missing leg are unusual problems. Sometimes resetting a head during the cementing process gives trouble. Usually figures are hollow and have hollow arms and legs. The head and neck can be reinforced from the inside with rolls of tough paper, a piece of balsa wood, or pieces of wood chosen to fit from a toy erector set. Also have handy a supply of probe sticks minus the cotton on the ends. Sometimes a French court figure needs a long gold-headed cane, or a shepherdess needs a crook. Once the probe stick is "enameled" or porcelainized, the substitution is perfect, and the need is fulfilled.

In general, arms and legs of figures should be doweled. However, tight cementing can be made to do the trick. If you decide to use dowels, you will have to grind anchor grooves. Resist grinding, because every time you grind, you have to repair the grind as well as make the initial repair. At times, of course, it is absolutely essential. Broken joins need strong repair support. Anchor grooves with strong cement are called for.

Restoring large, missing sections of a Dresden figure, whose garment or dress is spun porcelain lace, is done with china-mending powder—Porcelainate which is blended into System 4 (made up of Systems 2 and 4)—and when hard, it produces a beautiful, porcelain finish.

To make lace garments, use the finest netting you can buy. Cut the pieces to fit your need and when ready, dip them in the porcelain mix and apply to the areas under restoration. When dry, glaze the area, and recoat with a diluted mix of porcelainized Epoxyglass Resin and Hardener colored to the shade desired. Reglaze and paint with oil paints diluted or mixed with glaze.

Small-pointed brushes are needed for touching in eyelashes, eyebrows, and eyes, and the finest-pointed brush is needed to paint in lips and hair.

The repair of figurines is completed in much the same step-by-step sequence as the repair of other china.

step-by-step sequence

[1]   **Inspect the damaged figure for broken hands, arms, and legs; also for cracks and chips. These will have to be repaired in accordance with procedures for same given in Chapter 2.**

[2]   If your article has a broken hand and is chipped, cracked, and broken in more than three pieces, it may not be worth your time and the good materials it will take to restore it. A careful inspection will help you decide.

[3]   Plan assembly of the broken pieces.

[4]   Prepare strips of masking tape in lengths needed to secure the pieces to be fitted into the article.

[5]   Prepare the clay cement mix in equal parts.

[6]   Cement pieces into place in the article, secure with strips of masking tape from both the inside and the outside, and set aside to dry and harden.

[7]   Examine for uneven edges and displacement. The thickness of the material you use will determine the amount of displacement. If the pieces do not fit together perfectly, wait until cement has hardened, and grind off unevenness before removing masking tape.

[8]   After grinding away ragged edges, reexamine the figure carefully for chips.

[9]   Remove tapes.

[10]   If you have chips, you should also use the Epoxybond Putty Resin to fill the chips in, removing all excess.

[11]   Place in a sandbox, or balance in a bed of wax and allow to dry and harden.

[12]   Sand smooth any remaining rough edges.

[13]   If you have to mold a missing part of the figure, see Chapter 2 for instructions.

[14]   For finishing, cream the remainder of the clay until it can be applied with a soft art brush.

[15]   Apply creamy cement to the mended area, and blend it to a smooth join with surrounding surfaces.

[16]   Clean off excess. This is extremely important, because this clay cement mix will harden into a stone-hard substance, and once married to the article, it is almost impossible to remove it without marring the figure.

[17]   Remove rough edges with solvent, and in a feathering-out motion, reblend cement with surrounding areas.

[18]   Rebalance in the wax bed or sandbox, and let set and harden approximately 24 hours.

how to mend objets d'art, such as dogs, fruit, flowers, horses, lions, and similar pieces made of porcelain

Majolica. Usually a small dog of this kind and size suffers damage to paws, tail, ears, and nose, all of which are easily restored, given 20 to 30 minutes mending time, by using putty.

step-by-step sequence

[1]   **Inspect broken pieces for cracks and chips.**

[2]   **These will have to be repaired in accordance with procedures for same given in Chapter 2.**

[3]   Plan assembly of the broken pieces.

[4]   Prepare strips of masking tape in lengths needed to secure the pieces to be fitted into the article.

[5]   Prepare the cement mix, using System 3.

[6]   Cement pieces into place in the article, secure with strips of masking tape from both the inside and the outside, and set aside to dry and harden.

[7]   Examine for uneven edges and displacement. The thickness of the material you use will determine the amount of displacement. If the pieces do not fit together perfectly, wait until cement has hardened, and grind off unevenness before removing masking tape.

[8]   After grinding away ragged edges, reexamine for chips.

[9]   Remove tapes.

[10]   If you have chips, use the Porcelainate Cement Mix to fill in the chips, removing all excess.

[11]   Place in sandbox to dry and harden.

[12]   Sand any remaining rough edges smooth.

[13]   If you have multiple breaks, cement the pieces together as follows:

[14]   Grind a grid in the broken nubs on the article. You can put in a cross shape ("**X**") or a single groove if made deep enough.

[15]   The base cement mix should be firm. Press the cement into the grooves of the article's nubs.

[16]   Apply tape to secure in place.

[17]   Now cream the remainder of the mix until it can be applied with a soft art brush.

[18]   Apply creamy cement to the mended area, and blend it to a smooth join with surrounding surfaces.

[19]   Clean off excess.

[20]   Remove any rough edges, and in a feathering-out motion, reblend cement with surrounding areas.

[21]   Rebalance in the sandbox, and let set and harden for approximately 24 hours.

[22]   When cement is dry and hard, remove any excess film left by cement on surrounding surfaces with solvent. Film you can get off. Thick, hard cement will be virtually impossible to remove.

There are ways, of course; you can use a hard rubber polishing disc in a handgrinder.

[23]   Prepare epoxy porcelainizing mix, and blend in oil color to match article. Porcelainize mended surfaces.

[24]   Smooth until all edges and mends, as well as materials, are blended in with the body of the article.

[25]   Set aside to dry for 24 to 36 hours.

[26]   Decorate with oil paints mixed with New Gloss Glaze.

[27]   Finish glazing with New Gloss Glaze (System 5).

how to mend a china doll

statement of the problem

As you probably know, some dolls are easy to repair; others are quite difficult. Before attempting to restore a broken head, hand, or arm, it is well to find out what material you are dealing with. If you know that you are going to repair a German Greiner doll or a fine French doll signed by a famous maker, you can save time in selecting the right materials.

Broken china parts are only part of the problem. Has the doll been pulled or taken apart? Are the head, limbs, and body made of fine china material all broken? Can you work inside the body to repair it? These and many more questions will have to be answered as we mend the doll.

If the doll has more than sentimental value and is a rare antique, then it is indeed worth best efforts. So let us begin.

step-by-step sequence

[1]   Examine doll for spider cracks, and clean or boil all surfaces to be cemented together (porcelain or bisque only).

[2]   After boiling, cleanse under warm water with a stiff brush and soapsuds until free of bleaching solution (peroxide).

[3]   Plan the assembly of pieces.

[4]   Prepare cement. Mix thoroughly. Make a firm paste.

[5]   Prepare strips of masking tape, at least one for each two pieces.

[6]   Start to cement pieces together. Remove all excess cement.

[7]   Align and press together with exacting care.

[8]   Lay in a piece of aluminum foil to dry, or balance in sandbox.

[9]   Fill in nicks or small chips if any occur along the edges of cemented joins.

[10]   Set aside all pieces to dry for 24 hours.

[11]   Complete cementing when ready.

[12]   Balance article in sandbox.

[13]   When cement has hardened, again examine critically to determine materials for finish. If the doll is not a bisque doll, skip to Step 11 of the following step-by-step sequence.

If you have a bisque doll, the repairing procedure is not the same as given above, because you should use Epoxyglass Resin and Hardener. You now have the problem of achieving the right bisque finish and color. You do not ever glaze bisque.

[14]   Prepare a thinned solution of lacquer, and add color to match the doll or the areas surrounding the mend. Now add little pinches of plaster to the paint solution. (If you are professional, do not have the paint and plaster mixture any thicker than you usually use in an airbrush, or it won't pass through). The addition of plaster will flatten the lacquer to a bisque or satiny finish.

[15]   Apply mixture with a fine, soft, sable or camel's-hair brush. Apply a plain, uncolored paint solution of lacquer and plaster, layer after layer—Thin! Thin! Thin!—until all surfaces of the mended areas are covered. Make up small mixes of the same solution, add color, and bring the head, face, limbs, and body back to life with lifelike flesh tones.

how to mend the limbs and head of a jointed doll

China doll's head showing part of the head broken off before repair.

China doll's head after restoration.

step-by-step sequence

[1]   The elastic or rubber banding connecting the head and limbs has broken—use 1/8 inch wide elastic.

[2]   Cut the elastic into a length slightly longer than double the length of the doll's body.

[3]   Knot the loose ends of the elastic, and tie a square knot in the loop end, leaving a tight loop.

[4]   Insert the elastic knot end into the body through the neck opening. The knotted loop end should be sticking out at the top above the neck hole.

[5]   Stick a long nail through the loop and lay it across the opening so that the elastic cannot slip away from your fingers.

[6]   Pull the loose elastic ends out through the armholes, securely hook through the arm fasteners, and bring down through the leg holes. Repeat the process securing each limb so that it pulls in tight to the body.

[7]   Finally, hook the head on to the elastic loop. Remove the nail.

[8]   Carefully let the head snap down into place.

[9]   If head and limbs are not held tightly enough to the body, pull out the head, retie, and tighten the knot to shorten the loop.

[10]   Make final adjustments.

Now let us go back to painting and coloring, Step 13 of the previous stey-by-step sequence.

If doll is china, with glaze finish:

[11]   Remove all traces of cementing from mended surfaces. Use solvent such as acetone. If traces are very stubborn, I sometimes take my finest sandpaper, dip it in the acetone, and carefully brush off any disturbing traces of cement.

[12]   If the doll was jointed and is now joined together, head and limbs in place, you are now ready to invisibilize the repair.

[13]   Mix a base first application of oil paints with lacquer or New Gloss Glaze (boilproof) to match the basic areas to be painted. Thin the lacquer or glaze first. If this mixture does not have enough body to conceal the mends, add a pinch of Epoxybond White Resin to desired thickness. Recolor the mixture, because this is a white puttylike clay, and it will lighten the mix. This is used as an all-over blending.

[14]   Conceal all mended areas.

[15]   Feather-out and conceal mend. Smooth material out over the mended surfaces, blending it into the surrounding areas. (If you are professional and are using an airbrush, you may add this feathering-out procedure to your finishing techniques).

[16]   Mix additional small batches of color with lacquer oil paints and Epoxybond White Resin.

[17]   Apply where needed to restore doll's appearance to lifelike tones. You may use an airbrush or a brush. Use ever-so-light a touch of color to blend the final glow to satisfaction.

miracle-mending materials applied to glass

Glass is the miracle of turning sand into crystal by man's inventive genius. Like china, glass is made from a mixture of earth materials combined through centuries of man's experimentation to produce articles in a wide variety of forms and shapes for usefulness and beauty. Many such glass articles are fragile and easily broken. Broken and damaged glassware can be mended with the proper use of System 2, a two-part liquid substance, a miracle of the modern chemical laboratory.

The purpose of this chapter is to show how all glassware can be satisfactorily mended with System 2.

what is glass?

Glass is a substance composed chiefly of silica, which is obtained from a vitreous sand of the right grain and free from impurities. Other components are calcium oxide and several alkaline fluxes. Calcium oxide makes the glass resistant and constant, and enhances its brilliance. Alkaline fluxes such as sodium oxide and potassium oxide enable the glass to be melted and manipulated. These fluxes, with the addition of lime and sometimes lead oxide, give to glass an amorphous character—glass is not crystalline in structure, unlike rock crystal which it otherwise resembles closely.

how glass is made

Glass is made by fusing its components at high temperature into a fiery, molten liquid. This liquid is used in two principal ways to form objects of glassware: molding and blowing. Molding is by far the older process. A mold in the form of the exterior of the article to be made is first constructed, the interior being formed by a core. The molten glass is then carefully poured into the mold and allowed to cool.

As an intermediate step between molding and blowing, liquid glass was blown through a tube into prepared molds. A modern refinement of this ancient process is employed today in the mass production of glass bottles.

Glassblowing is a technique requiring a high degree of skill. Glass in a thickening liquid state can be "gathered" on the end of a long, hollow tube and, by man's breath, blown into a round bubble. This is the first step in making an article of blown glassware. As the bubble is reheated and swung at the end of the blowpipe, a cylinder is formed. At the precise state of soft, pliable firmness, the cylinder is transferred from the end of the blowpipe to a pontil (rod). Thereafter, it is maintained in this condition to be cut with shears and manipulated into the required shape.

All articles of glassware were made by these two processes until the invention in the latter part of the 17th century of a way to make flat or plate glass for commercial purposes.

different kinds of glass

There are three principal kinds of glass:

1. *Ornate crystalware* (commercial types).
    Soda-lime glass is soft and easy to melt, relatively easy to manipulate, and is pure and clear. It lends itself to a variety of decorative techniques, such as trailing glass rods on glass surfaces to produce raised effects, that are rarely attempted with other types of glass.

2. *Crystal stemware and table services*
    Potash-lime glass is less fusible, very hard and less malleable, but very brilliant.

3. *Cut-glass.*
    Potash-lead (or flint) glass is softer and easier to melt, but much heavier. It has greater brilliance and a high refractive index. It breaks up rays of light into the colors of the rainbow. This type of glass is used for cut-glass articles.

In addition to crystal-clear glass, there are a number of varieties of glass which when broken require different mending techniques (see Appendix). These types of glass are produced by adding metal oxides to the mass before or during fusion. One of the most beautiful effects is achieved by the addition of colloidal silver, which produces a copper-oxide red color. Colloidal gold is also used.

Bone-glass is made by adding bone ash to the molten mass. Milk glass is opaque and is produced through the admixture of felspar-fluorspar. Opaline effects are achieved by thinning the milk-glass mixture. Opaque and opaline glass require a combination of System 1 and System 2 for mending.

how to mend clear
glass articles (crystal)

HOW TO MEND A BROKEN CRYSTAL
CANDLESTICK WITH MISSING CHIPS:
*Step 1—Candlestick is balanced in a sandbox
(any baking pan will do) filled with white
fishtank sand obtainable at any pet store.*

*Step 2—Mix epoxies of System 2, adding a
slight touch of blue or green coloring to match
crystal.*

Step 3—Apply material with a brush, drop by drop.

Step 4—Coat the mend with additional brushed-on Epoxy-glass mix.

Step 5—Remove the excess with a razor blade dampened in lacquer thinner.

134

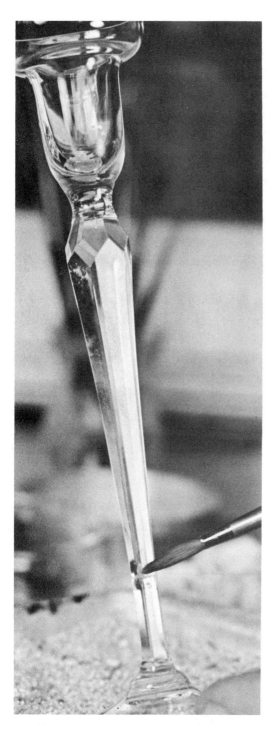

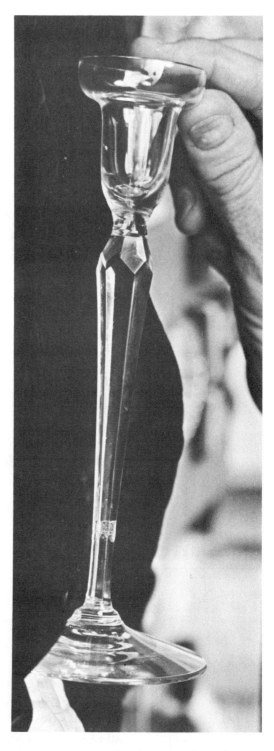

Step 6—Coat with Epoxyglass mix over,
above, and below mended areas. Recoat
between drying and hardening time.

Step 7—Examine for clearness of mend.

step-by-step sequence

[1]   Classify damages (flake chips, lip or edge chips, missing parts, cracks, or multiple breaks).

[2]   Use, but only if absolutely necessary, handgrinder and carborundum disc (made of diamond dust). Warm pieces first, then place the article under faucet drip of warm water, and grind in anchor grooves. If you grind, the mend will show.

[3]   To make a mold for a missing part in an article of dinnerware, heat sheet wax, and make a mold.

[4]   Clean the surfaces of the damaged pieces.

[5]   Apply mold material. If you use a plastic mold, mixture should be made of equal parts.

[6]   Apply plastic mix with a spatula, permitting time of 8 minutes.

[7]   Prepare Epoxyglass Resin and Hardener. Fill the mold with mixture. Permit to harden.

[8]   Remove molded piece, and cement into place with additional epoxy mixture.

[9]   The repaired area can be glazed with a coat of New Gloss Glaze. When it is dry, additional thin coats of epoxy mix may be added with a feathering-out motion.

[10] Dampen your fingers in solvent and then in the epoxy mix to perfect this feathering-out technique.

how to mend colored glass articles

step-by-step sequence

[1]   Grind in anchor grooves.

[2]   Make a wax or plastic mold.

[3]   If only a wax back-up mold is required, fasten it in place with tape.

[4]   Prepare Epoxyglass White Resin Finishing Paste. Mix with Epoxyglass Resin and Hardener. Color mix to match the article.

[5]   Build walls of masking tape, fill damaged area with the colored mixture, and set aside to harden.

[6]   Fill when hard. Remove tape. Smooth with razor blade until repair is smooth and even with all surrounding edges.

[7]   Set in oven to dry and harden.

[8]   When hard, apply a coat of sizing liquid. Heat dry in an oven set at about 140 degrees.

[9]   Sand any unevenness away, reglaze, and reheat.

[10]   Prepare epoxyglass mix. Add oil color paints to match the article. Add white for body and opaqueness. Finalize color to match.

[11]   Feather-out applied mix until repair is completely invisibilized and material is perfectly blended with surrounding surfaces.

[12]   Lightly spray with clear glaze.

[13]   Decorate. Lastly, if required, apply gold leaf.

[14]   Burnish as desired.

how to mend a bowl (cereal, salad, soup, sugar, vegetable, fruit, or punch)

step-by-step sequence

[1]   Inspect damaged pieces for cracks and chips.

[2]   These will have to be repaired in accordance with procedures for same given under their respective headings in Chapter 2.

[3]   Plan assembly of the broken pieces.

[4]   Prepare strips of masking tape in lengths needed to secure the pieces to be fitted into the article.

[5]   Prepare the Epoxyglass Resin Mix in equal parts.

[6]   Cement pieces into place in the article, secure with strips of masking tape from both the inside and the outside, and set aside to dry and harden.

[7]   Examine for uneven edges and displacement. The thickness of the material you use will determine the amount of displacement. If pieces do not fit together perfectly, wait until cement has hardened, warm pieces, and polish off unevenness before removing masking tape.

[8]   After polishing away ragged edges, reexamine for chips.

[9]   Remove tapes.

[10]   If you have chips, you should use Epoxyglass Resin to fill in the chips, one layer at a time. Remove all excess.

[11]   Place in sandbox or wax bed to dry and harden.

[12]   Polish any remaining rough edges smooth with soft rubber disc.

[13]   If you have to build a missing piece, cement the broken pieces together. Let harden.

[14]   Warm pieces to be cemented. Apply a sheet of wax mold to the underside, and secure with masking tape.

[15]   The epoxy cement should be thick. Apply the cement with an art brush to get into the breaks and fill the gaps.

[16]   If necessary, apply tape to the inside and outside edges of the piece, and stand it on edge in sandbox to fill in the missing part.

[17]   Remove excess. After the fill has set, if you need more epoxy, apply it evenly all around the mend with a soft art brush dipped in thinner.

[18]   As you apply the cement to the mended area, blend it with thinner until you obtain a smooth join with the surrounding surfaces.

[19]   Clean off excess. This is extremely important, because this epoxy cement mix will harden into a glasslike substance, and once married to your article, is almost impossible to remove without damage to appearance.

[20]   Remove any rough edges by adding a thin coat of epoxy cement, and in a feathering-out motion, reblend with surrounding areas.

[21]   Rebalance in the sandbox or wax bed, and let set and harden for approximately 24 hours.

[22]   When epoxy cement is dry and hard, remove with a razor blade any excess film left by cement on surrounding surfaces. Film you can get off. Hardened epoxy mixes will be virtually impossible to remove or polish without damage to appearance. There are ways, of course; one way is to keep your work to a fine finish at each stage as you go. You may remedy bad effects with glaze, but it is a remedy, not a cure.

[23]   To decorate or porcelainize glass, prepare epoxyglass mix, and blend in oil color to match article. Apply to mended surfaces.

[24]   Smooth until all edges and mends, as well as materials, are blended in with the body of the article.

[25]   Set aside to dry for 24 to 36 hours.

[26]   Decorate with oil paints and glaze.

[27]   Finish glazing.

how to mend
a creamer

step-by-step sequence

[1]   Inspect damaged pieces for broken spout, handle, or cracks and chips.

[2]   These will have to be repaired in accordance with procedures for same given in Chapter 2.

[3]   Plan assembly of the broken pieces.

[4]   Prepare strips of masking tape in lengths needed to secure the pieces to be fitted into the article.

[5]   Prepare your cement mix in equal parts.

[6]   Cement pieces into place in the article, secure with strips of masking tape from both the inside and the outside, and set aside to dry and harden.

[7]   Examine for uneven edges and displacement. The thickness of the material you use will determine the amount of displacement. If the pieces do not fit together perfectly, wait until cement has hardened, warm your pieces, and polish off unevenness before removing masking tape.

[8]   After polishing away ragged edges, reexamine the piece carefully for chips.

[9]   Remove tapes.

[10]   If you have chips, you should use a thick epoxy cement mix to fill in the chips, one layer at a time. Remove all excess.

[11]   Place in sandbox or wax bed to dry and harden.

[12]   Polish any remaining rough edges on the piece smooth with soft rubber disc.

[13]   If you have to put on a broken handle, cement the pieces together. Let harden.

[14]   Warm pieces to be cemented.

[15]   The epoxy cement should be thick. Apply the cement with an art brush to get into the breaks of the article's nubs and into the handle.

[16]   Apply tape to inside of article, and bring a long-enough piece of it out over the edge to secure the handle in place.

[17]   Now remove excess. If you need more epoxy, apply it evenly all around the mend with a soft art brush dipped in thinner.

[18]   As you apply the cement to the mended area, blend it with thinner until you obtain a smooth join with handle and surrounding surfaces.

[19]   Clean off excess. This is extremely important, because this epoxy cement mix will harden into a glasslike substance, and once married to your article, is almost impossible to remove without damage to appearance.

[20]   Remove any rough edges by adding a thin coat of epoxy cement, and in a feathering-out motion, reblend with surrounding areas.

[21]   Rebalance in sandbox or wax bed, and let set and harden for approximately 24 hours.

[22]   When epoxy cement is dry and hard, remove with a razor blade any excess film left by cement on surrounding surfaces. You can get film off. A thick, hard epoxy will be virtually impossible to remove or polish without damage to appearance. There are ways, of course; you can keep your work to a fine finish at each stage as you go. You may remedy bad effects with New Gloss Glaze, but it is a remedy, not a cure.

[23]   To decorate or porcelainize milk glass, prepare epoxy porcelainizing mix, and blend in oil color to match article. Apply to mended surfaces.

[24]   Smooth until all edges and mends, as well as materials, are blended in with the body of the article.

[25]   Set aside to dry for 24 to 36 hours.

[26]   Decorate with oil paints mixed with New Gloss Glaze.

[27]   Finish glazing with New Gloss Glaze.

[28]   To mold the lip of your creamer, apply tape to a wax mold. Mold warm wax to shape lip, and secure with tape. Fill in broken lip area with epoxy until you obtain a smooth join with lip edges. Set aside to harden. Remove wax mold and tape. Glaze with New Gloss Glaze. If necessary, add additional layers of epoxy cement, and reglaze.

how to mend a glass decanter

*Sketches of cut and engraved nineteenth
century decanters and rummers.*

step-by-step sequence

[1]   Inspect damaged pieces for broken stopper, or cracks and chips.

[2]   These will have to be repaired in accordance with procedures for same given under their respective headings in Chapter 2.

[3]   Plan assembly of the broken pieces.

[4]   Prepare strips of masking tape in lengths needed to secure the pieces to be fitted into the article.

[5]   Prepare cement mix in equal parts, using System 2.

[6]   Cement pieces into place in the article, secure with strips of mask-

ing tape from both the inside and the outside, and set aside to dry and harden.

[7]   Examine for uneven edges and displacement. The thickness of the material you use will determine the amount of displacement. If the pieces do not fit together perfectly, wait until cement has hardened, warm your pieces, and polish off unevenness before removing masking tape.

[8]   After polishing away ragged edges, reexamine for chips.

[9]   Remove tapes.

[10]   If you have chips, you should use a thick epoxy cement mix of equal parts to fill in the chips, one layer at a time. Remove all excess.

[11]   Place in a sandbox or wax bed to dry and harden.

[12]   Polish any remaining rough edges smooth with soft rubber disc.

[13]   If you have to mend a broken stopper, cement the pieces together. Let harden.

[14]   Warm pieces to be cemented.

[15]   The epoxy cement should be thick. Apply the cement with an art brush to get into the breaks of the article's nub.

[16]   Apply tape to inside of article and bring a long-enough piece of it out over the top and bottom to secure the mend in place.

[17]   Remove excess. Later on, if you need more epoxy, apply it evenly all around the mend with a soft art brush dipped in thinner.

[18]   As you apply the cement to the mended area, blend it with thinner until you obtain a smooth join with surrounding surfaces.

[19]   Clean off excess. This is extremely important, because this epoxy cement mix will harden into a glasslike substance, and once married to your article, is almost impossible to remove without damage to appearance.

[20]   Remove any rough edges by adding a thin coat of epoxy cement, and in a feathering-out motion, reblend with surrounding areas.

[21]   Rebalance in sandbox or wax bed, and let set and harden for approximately 24 hours.

[22]   When epoxy cement is dry and hard, remove with a razor blade any excess film left by cement on surrounding surfaces. You can get film off. A thick, hard epoxy will be virtually impossible to remove or polish without damage to appearance. There are ways, of course; one way is to keep your work to a fine finish at each

stage as you go. You may remedy bad effects with New Gloss Glaze, but it is a remedy, not a cure.

[23]   To decorate or porcelainize milk glass or art glass, prepare epoxy mix, and blend in oil color to match article. Apply to mended surfaces.

[24]   Smooth until all edges and mends, as well as materials, are blended in with the body of the article.

[25]   Set aside to dry for 24 to 36 hours.

[26]   Decorate with oil paints and New Gloss Glaze.

[27]   Finish glazing with New Gloss Glaze.

how to mend candlesticks
made of clear crystal

step-by-step sequence

[1]   Classify damage (flake chip, lip or edge chip, missing part, crack, or multiple breaks). See Chapter 2 for applicable step sequences.

[2]   Clean all surfaces thoroughly. Boil to loosen all foreign substances, old glue, or old mending materials.

[3]   If you have to make a mold for a missing part, heat or warm a sheet of wax until pliable, and make a mold. Or:

[4]   If you prefer using plastic molding material, mix according to directions, equal parts, and let set for about 8 minutes on the area that you are making an impression of. Remove, and fill the mold with cement mixture.

[5]   Apply the mold in place, secure, and set aside to harden over night.

[6]   When molded material is hard, smooth edges with a carbide rubber wheel set in a handgrinder. Use *Scotch Tape* to hold in place while repair cement is hardening.

[7]   Apply one or two coats of New Gloss Glaze. Let dry. Recoat with epoxy cement mix. Feather-out the epoxy cement until it is perfectly blended with surrounding surfaces.

[8]   Reglaze repaired area with New Gloss Glaze. This substance can also be feathered-out. The repair should be invisible or almost

so. In any case, it will be as nearly perfect as is professionally possible.

how to mend opaque art glass

step-by-step sequence

[1]   Classify damage (flake chip, lip or edge chip, missing part, crack, multiple breaks).

[2]   Clean all surfaces thoroughly. Boil to loosen all foreign substances, old glue, or old mending materials.

[3]   If you have to make a mold for a missing part, heat or warm a sheet of wax until pliable, and make a mold. Or:

[4]   Use plastic mold. Mix according to directions, equal parts, and let set for about 8 minutes on the area of which you are making an impression. Remove, and fill the mold with cement mixture. Color may be added to match the color of the article you are mending. If you are mending milk glass, be sure you get the exact shade of white—as there are many different shades. Also, mix the color into the cement powder and hardener very gradually to get a smooth blend. Use Systems 2 and 4.

[5]   Fill the mold with the mixture, and set aside to harden 24 to 36 hours.

[6]   When molded material is hard, remove from mold, and smooth edges with a carbide rubber wheel set in a handgrinder. Cement in place.

how to mend opaque art glass bottles (blown or molded)

Any opaque glass can be simulated with use of china cement powder mix or white putty. Problems will arise in matching colors and surfaces, but the following materials will do the job if properly applied.

step-by-step sequence

[1]   Classify damage (flake chip, lip or edge chip, missing part, crack,

or multiple breaks). Study sequences given in Chapter 2 for any of these types of repairs.

[2]   Clean all surfaces thoroughly. Boil to loosen all foreign substances, old glue, or old mending materials.

[3]   If you have to make a mold for a missing part, heat or warm a sheet of wax until pliable, and make a mold. Or:

[4]   Use plastic mold. Mix according to directions, equal parts, and let set for about 8 minutes on the area that you are making an impression of. Remove, and fill the mold with cement mixture. Color may be added to match the color of the article you are mending. If you are mending milk glass or satin glass, be sure to get the exact shade, because there are many different shades of color. Also, mix the color into cement powder and hardener very gradually to get a smooth blend, or bisque finish.

[5]   Fill and apply the mold in place, secure, and set aside to harden 24 to 36 hours.

[6]   When the molded material is hard, remove from mold, and smooth edges with a carbide rubber wheel set in a handgrinder. Cement in place. Use masking tape for support or a wax mold for back-up to hold material in place while mending-cement is hardening.

[7]   Apply one or two coats of New Gloss Glaze to mended area. Let set and dry.

[8]   Remove tapes and/or wax back-up support. Smooth with soft rubber disc. Apply one or two coats of New Gloss Glaze.

[9]   Make a mix of Epoxyglass cement of equal parts. Add color to White Resin Paste or to the epoxy itself to match article. Get exact shade by matching in daylight. Coat mended areas with the epoxy mix. Feather-out the epoxy cement until it is perfectly blended with all surrounding areas.

[10]   Apply final glaze.

how to mend opaque glass (general procedure)

step-by-step sequence

[1]   Classify damage (flake chip, lip or edge chip, missing part, crack, or multiple breaks). See Chapter 2 for step sequences under applicable headings.

[2]   Clean all surfaces thoroughly. Boil to loosen all foreign sub-
       stances, old glue, or old mending materials.

[3]   If you have to make a mold for a missing part, heat or warm until
       pliable a sheet of wax, and make a mold. Or:

[4]   Use plastic mold. Mix according to directions, equal parts, and let
       set for about 8 minutes on the area of which you are making an
       impression. Remove, and fill the mold with cement mixture. Color
       may be added to match the color of the article you are mending.
       If you are mending milk glass, be sure you get the exact shade of
       white, because there are many different shades of white. Also,
       mix the color into the cement powder and hardener very gradually
       to get a smooth blend.

[5]   Apply the mold in place with the mixture and set aside to harden
       for 24 to 36 hours.

[6]   When molded material is hard, remove from the mold, and smooth
       edges with a carbide rubber wheel set in a handgrinder. Use
       Scotch Tape for support for back-up to hold material in place
       while mending cement is hardening.

[7]   Apply one or two coats of New Gloss Glaze to mended area. Let
       set and dry.

[8]   Remove tape and/or back-up support. Smooth with soft rubber
       disc. Apply one or two coats of New Gloss Glaze.

[9]   Make a mix of Epoxyglass resin cement of equal parts. Add color
       to match article. Get exact shade by matching in daylight. Coat
       mended areas with the epoxy cement mix. Feather-out the epoxy
       cement until it is perfectly blended with all surrounding areas.

[10]   Reglaze with New Gloss Glaze. Set aside to cure, and when dry
       and hard, decorate to design. Gold, after glazing: Glaze sprayed
       on top of gold will turn it a bronze cast.

how to mend opaque
glass candlesticks

step-by-step sequence

[1]   Inspect damaged pieces for broken handle or cracks and chips.
       These will have to be repaired in accordance with procedures for
       same given in Chapter 2.

[2]   If your article has a broken handle and is chipped, cracked, and
       broken in more than three pieces, it may not be worth your time

and the good materials it will take to restore it. A careful inspection will help you decide.

[3]   Plan assembly of the broken pieces.

[4]   Prepare strips of masking tape in lengths needed to secure the pieces to be fitted into the article.

[5]   Prepare cement mix in equal parts, using Systems 2 and 4.

[6]   Cement pieces into place in the article, secure with strips of masking tape from both the inside and the outside, and set aside to dry and harden.

[7]   Examine for uneven edges and displacement. The thickness of the material you use will determine the amount of displacement. If the pieces do not fit together perfectly, wait until cement has hardened, and grind off unevenness before removing masking tape.

[8]   After grinding away ragged edges, reexamine for chips.

[9]   Remove tapes.

[10]   If you have chips, you should use Epoxybond Putty Resin and Hardener to fill in the chips, removing all excess.

[11]   Place in sandbox, or balance in a bed of wax to dry and harden.

[12]   Sand smooth any remaining rough edges.

[13]   If you have to put on a broken handle, cement the pieces together. Let harden. Use System 2.

[14]   Grind a grid in the top and bottom nubs of the article, and grind grooves in top and bottom of handle. You can put in a cross shape ("**X**") or a single groove.

[15]   The base cement should be firm. Press the cement into the grooves of the article's nubs and into the handle.

[16]   Apply tape to inside of article, and bring a long-enough piece of it out over the edge to secure the handle in place.

[17]   Now cream the remainder of the mix until it can be applied with a soft art brush, using System 4 colored to match.

[18]   Apply creamy cement to the mended area, and blend it to a smooth join with handle and surrounding surfaces.

[19]   Clean off excess. This is extremely important, because this clay cement mix will harden into a stone-hard substance, and once married to your article, is almost impossible to remove.

[20]   Remove any rough edges with razor blade, and in a feathering-out motion, reblend cement with surrounding areas.

[21]   **Rebalance in wax bed or sandbox, and let set and harden approximately 24 hours.**

[22]   **When cement is dry and hard, remove with a razor blade any excess film left by cement on surrounding surfaces. Film you can get off. Thick, hard cement will be virtually impossible to remove. There are ways, of course; you can use a hard rubber polishing wheel in handgrinder. Sandpaper is apt to scratch surrounding surfaces and do additional glaze damage to mended surfaces.**

[23]   **Smooth until all edges and mends, as well as materials, are blended in with the body of the article.**

[24]   **Set aside to dry for 24 to 36 hours.**

[25]   **Decorate with oil paints and New Gloss Glaze.**

[26]   **Finish glazing with New Gloss Glaze.**

how to mend cabinet pieces

Cabinet pieces are usually heirlooms or articles you have collected. You are aware of their value. Almost all collections of such articles consist of European or Oriental porcelain articles and frequently contain rare specimens of American glass. Among such collections, you will find an aggregate of Art Glass bowls, cameo glass, creamers, cups, Christmas plates, dolls and figures, and groups in porcelain of all kinds—Early American blown glass, pattern glass goblets, paperweights, teapots, coffeepots, animals in both porcelain and glass, and many other articles—that may be classified either as tableware or as decorative accessories.

Each of these ornamental or decorative articles may be identified as one that has already been discussed under its proper name or heading, and the step sequences applicable to the type of repair involved have been given under these headings.

However, if you have not looked further, the materials and equipment listed here are the only kind you can use to achieve a professional mending result. Your collection will probably come under the heading of glass or china. Unusual collections of articles such as fans may also be identified in accordance with categories of damage and/or the composition of the article. The applicable materials for glass or china apply.

General step sequences are given here for clear and opaque glass, as well as for the various damages that can occur to a fine article of porcelain. These sequences are not intended to repeat details of mending given in Chapter 2 or Chapter 3, which are applicable to a specific type of mend. They are meant to be correlated, and it is recommended you study both.

how to mend cabinet pieces of clear glass (crystal)

step-by-step sequence

[1] Classify damage (flake chip, lip or edge chip, missing part, crack, or multiple breaks).

[2] Clean all surfaces thoroughly. Boil to loosen all foreign substances, old glue, or old mending materials.

[3] If you have to make a mold for a missing part, heat or warm until pliable a sheet of wax, and make a mold. Or:

[4] If you prefer using plastic molding material, mix according to directions, equal parts, and let set for about 8 minutes on the area that you are making an impression of. Remove, and fill the mold with cement mixture.

[5] Apply the mold in place securely, and set aside to harden over night.

[6] When molded material is hard, smooth edges with a carbide rubber wheel set in a handgrinder. Use *Scotch Tape* or a wax back-up mold to hold in place while repair cement is hardening.

[7] Apply one or two coats of New Gloss Glaze. Let dry. Recoat with Epoxyglass cement mix. Feather-out the epoxy cement until it is perfectly blended with surrounding surfaces. Tint your mix.

[8] Reglaze repaired area with New Gloss Glaze. This substance can also be feathered-out. The repair should be invisible or almost so. In any case, it will be as nearly perfect as is professionally possible.

how to mend cabinet pieces of opaque glass

step-by-step sequence

[1] Classify any damaged pieces for broken spout, handle, or cracks and chips. These will have to be repaired in accordance with procedures for same given in Chapter 2.

[2]   Clean all surfaces thoroughly. Boil to loosen all foreign substances, old glue, or old mending materials.

[3]   If you have to make a mold for a missing part, heat or warm until pliable a sheet of wax, and make a mold. Or:

[4]   Use plastic mold. Mix according to directions, equal parts, and let set for about 8 minutes on the area of which you are making an impression. Remove, and fill the mold with cement mixture. Color may be added to match the color of the article you are mending. If you are mending milk glass, be sure you get the exact shade of white. Also, mix the color into cement powder and hardener very gradually to get a smooth blend.

[5]   Apply the mold with the mixture in place, secure, and set aside to harden 24 to 36 hours.

[6]   When molded material is hard, remove from mold, and smooth edges with a carbide rubber wheel set in a handgrinder. Use tape for support or a wax mold for back-up to hold material in place while mending cement is hardening.

[7]   Apply one or two coats of New Gloss Glaze to mended area. Let set and dry.

[8]   Remove tapes and/or wax back-up support. Smooth with soft rubber disc. Apply one or two coats of New Gloss Glaze.

[9]   Make a mix of Epoxyglass Resin cement of equal parts. Add color to match article. Get exact shade by matching in daylight. Coat mended areas with the epoxy cement mix. Feather-out epoxy cement until it is perfectly blended with all surrounding areas.

[10]   Reglaze with New Gloss Glaze. Set aside to cure, and when dry and hard, decorate to design. Gold after glaze—glaze sprayed on top of gold will turn it a bronze cast.

how to mend opaque
glass objets d'art

step-by-step sequence

[1]   Inspect broken pieces for cracks and chips. These will have to be repaired in accordance with procedures for same given under respective headings in Chapter 2.

[2]   If your article is chipped, cracked, and broken in more than three pieces, you will have to decide on its value to you. As far as

mending is concerned, it may not be worth your time and the good materials it will take to restore it. A careful inspection will help you decide.

[3]   Plan assembly of the two or three broken pieces.

[4]   Prepare strips of masking tape in lengths needed to secure the pieces to be fitted into the article.

[5]   Prepare Epoxyglass cement mix in equal parts.

[6]   Cement pieces into place, secure with strips of masking tape from both the inside and the outside, and set aside to dry and harden.

[7]   Examine for uneven edges and displacement. The thickness of the material you use will determine the amount of displacement. If the pieces do not fit together perfectly, wait until cement has hardened, and grind off unevenness before removing masking tape.

[8]   After grinding away ragged edges, reexamine for chips.

[9]   Remove tapes.

[10]   If you have chips, you should use the porcelainate cement to fill in the chips, removing all excess cement.

[11]   Place in sandbox to dry and harden.

[12]   Sand any remaining rough edges until smooth.

[13]   If you have multiple breaks, cement the pieces together with System 2 as follows:

[14]   Grind a grid in the nubs of the article. Grooves should be in the shape of an "X" and about 1/4 inch deep.

[15]   Your base cement should be firm. Press the cement into the grooves and into the nubs.

[16]   Apply clear *Scotch Tape* to the article to secure the pieces you are cementing on and to add support at vital points. Keep them at the right angle. Set aside to dry and harden.

[17]   Now cream the System 1 mix until it can be applied with a soft art brush. Blend to a smooth join with all surrounding surfaces.

[18]   Apply a finishing coat of creamed cement, tinted to match.

[19]   Clean off excess, and set aside to harden.

[20]   Remove any rough edges with solvent and a razor blade while cement is firm but not hard, and again feather-out and reblend cement.

[21]   Rebalance in sandbox, and let set and harden for approximately 24 hours.

[22]   When cement is dry and hard, remove with solvent any excess film left by cement on surrounding surfaces. Film you can get off. Thick, hard cement will be virtually impossible to remove. There are ways, of course; you can use a hard rubber polishing disc in a handgrinder.

[23]   Prepare epoxy mix, and blend in oil color to match the article.

[24]   Smooth all edges and mends, as well as materials, until they blend in with the body of the article.

[25]   Set aside to dry for 24 to 36 hours.

[26]   Decorate with oil paints and New Gloss Glaze.

chapter five

---

miracle-mending
materials
applied to
stoneware and pottery

The history of pottery is a long, absorbing story beginning as primitive man everywhere started using the clay under his feet to produce articles for his domestic use.

The problem of present-day owners of pottery, whether these are rare treasures from the past or pieces of a modern table service, is that pottery is often broken and damaged. The purpose of this chapter is to show how all types of broken and damaged pottery can be properly mended, repaired, and restored to normal use.

information about stoneware and pottery

Whieldon or pottery teapot. Worth repair, this piece can be restored quickly and easily with adhesive putty. The handle and finial have been hand-molded and applied (see instructions in Chapter 2 for making a cup handle).

what is pottery?

Pottery is a ware shaped from clay. Clay is a fine-grained form of natural material, malleable when wet, that contains primarily hydrated silicates of aluminum. Articles of this material, after being formed, are heat-treated at varying temperatures in their manufacture. The mending materials used on broken or damaged pottery require no firing, although when set and hardened, they become stonelike.

Two types of pottery: While there are as many types of decorations on pottery as there have been artisans through the centuries to devise them—from the elaborately enameled and bejeweled pottery of ancient China to the colorful patterns of Pennsylvania-German slipware and sgraffito—there are only two types of pottery the mender needs to know about for mending purposes. These are soft-paste earthenware, which has a high lime content, and hard-paste earthenware containing no lime (see Appendix). In composition and thickness of the body, hard-paste earthenware is often similar to stoneware and porcelain.

what is stoneware?

The simplest form of pottery is earthenware, which is merely baked clay. When it is baked at a very high temperature, the clay melts into a solid mass impervious to liquids. This is stoneware. The Chinese, about 100 B.C., made some excellent stoneware that was glazed with a rich yellow and leaf-green.

In Europe, Germany took the lead in the 12th and 13th centuries in making stoneware. It was peculiar to the country, because it was made of pipeclay found chiefly in the Rhineland. The clay was mixed with felspar, quartz, and fireclay, generally used for making firebricks and crucibles, and the articles were given only one firing. Often handfuls of salt were thrown into the kiln at its greatest heat to produce salt-glaze stoneware.

soft-paste pottery

In England particularly, where there was a great demand for table services, most of which were white salt-glaze stoneware, the commercial potters began searching for a cheap but durable substitute that could be more easily manufactured than stoneware.

Josiah Wedgwood, who was well-established in the pottery business, discovered a new material that came to be known as Queens Ware. It looked expensive, was easy to make, was durable but considerably lighter in weight than stoneware, and was comparatively cheap. Under the patronage of Queen Charlotte, this ware became popular, and in a short time, drove salt-glaze stoneware off the market.

how to mend stoneware,
a hard-paste type
of pottery

Stoneware articles are vitreous. A vitreous article is iron-hard (and may be called ironstone), because it is full of fine particles of glossy, granitelike crystals of petuntse, an iron-strong binder.

composition of the article

It is important to recognize whether the kind of ware you are going to mend is chinaware or stoneware, because you may find it well to use more of a glass-mending type material than a china-mending material.

Your most difficult problem will be to finish off the edges of the repair so that they correspond or blend into the surrounding areas of your broken article.

weight of the broken pieces

In any broken article you must also consider the weight of the broken pieces. The technique of having a stoneware mend "hold" is a different technique than that used for a light-weight piece of chinaware. When you think of chinaware, you at once associate it with a substance that is light in weight, possibly fragile. This is not the case with stoneware.

Stoneware, of course, may be made to look fragile and lovely (Wedgwood being among the most beautiful of such ware) but stoneware or earthenware is indeed heavier, tougher, harder to break, and more durable.

However, durability may be downgraded a bit when you consider how much easier it is to chip than to break. Naturally, the closer the relation of the article to glass, that is, the more glass it has in it, the easier it will be to flake off a chip.

suitability of the mending material

Any of the damages are going to be a challenge when it comes to grinding. Grinding in anchor-type grooves, "X"s, grids, or footers is difficult and tedious with stoneware. It would be wise to have good quality carborundum (diamond dust) cutting discs, and do any grinding under a spigot of dripping water to keep down the dust when cutting into ironstone or stoneware.

The alternative is to avoid grinding if the damage is one you can repair without this unpleasant operation.

When you have classified the damage of the article as a flake chip, rim chip, or a missing part, grind in the anchoring grid, and select the type of mending material most compatible with the type of stoneware article you are mending.

repair of the damage with a view to the finish

For stoneware that has been made to look like a light buff clay, you would ordinarily select Epoxybond Resin Putty and Hardener to restore the damage.

If the damage has occurred to a piece of white ironstone, it would be well to select Porcelainate mix. Of course, if an entire piece is missing, not just a chip, you will have to fill in the area with clay cement mixture and use a back-up mold of wax secured by masking tape.

When the clay mix has hardened, apply surface coat to match or blend with surrounding areas. The matching or blending coat may very well be of a different mix of materials.

bisque finish

If the article is Wedgwood, you will have a bisque finish to achieve. Turn to the section on Finishes in Chapter 6 for Bisque.

white ceramic finish

If your article is white ironstone, you will want to use Epoxyglass Resin mix with a matching shade of white. The shade and thickness of the "porcelain" mix can be determined by the amount of white oil color and the Epoxyglass Resin White Finishing Paste that you may add to the epoxy mix.

how to mend a stoneware teapot

You will have to consider the size and shape of your teapot before you begin to mend it. Chances are the handle is broken off, and this can be bad news. A strong handle is vital to the use of your teapot. When you repair the handle or make a new one, it would be well to wire-wind the entire handle, and then porcelainize over it to give it added strength.

statement of the problem

Usually there are nubs projecting from the back of the pot left where the handle was attached. If you have no handle or a badly broken one, it would be well to make a new one. The nubs on your old handle will give you a clue as to how large a handle you will need. Shape or design should harmonize with that of the teapot. A figure "5" is a good design.

Cut a pattern from paper until you achieve one nearly like the original in size and shape, or mold one from soft wax, and duplicate it by executing the design in Epoxybond Resin cement mix. It is not hard to design a handle that is appropriate.

If you decide to mend the broken handle, and have the pieces to do so, the wire may be copper or aluminum. In any case, it should be flexible-enough to permit an easy wind around the cemented pieces.

Soft molding wax is obtainable in bulk from your local hardware store. You will want at least a pound or two because it provides good support for molds and for back-up when a missing piece has to be filled in.

These materials can be stored in a cupboard until needed again. They remain usable over a period of years.

step-by-step sequence

[1]   Inspect damaged pieces for broken lid, spout, finial, handle, or cracks and chips. These will have to be repaired in accordance with procedures for same given under their respective headings in Chapter 2.

[2]   If your article has a broken handle and is chipped, cracked, and broken into more than three pieces, you will have to decide on its value to you. As far as mending is concerned, unless the article is an antique or a collectors' item, it may not be worth the time and good materials it will take to restore it. A careful inspection will help you decide.

[3]   Plan assembly of the broken pieces.

[4]   Prepare strips of masking tape in lengths needed to secure the pieces to be fitted into the article.

[5]   Prepare cement mix in equal parts.

[6]   Cement pieces into place in the article, secure with strips of masking tape from both the inside and the outside, and set aside to dry and harden.

[7]   Examine for uneven edges and displacement. The thickness of the material you use will determine the amount of displacement. If the pieces do not fit together prefectly, wait until cement has hardened, and grind off unevenness before removing masking tape.

[8]   After grinding away ragged edges, reexamine for chips.

[9]   Remove tapes.

[10]   If you have chips, you should use Porcelainate mix to fill in the chips, removing all excess.

[11]   Place in sandbox to dry and harden.

[12]   Sand smooth any remaining rough edges.

[13]   If you have to put on a broken handle, cement the pieces together. Let harden.

[14]   Grind a grid in the top and bottom nubs on the article, and grind grooves in top and bottom of handle. You can put in a cross shape ("**X**") or a single groove.

[15]   Mix Epoxybond Resin Putty and Hardener. The cement should be firm. Press the cement into the grooves of the article's nubs and into the handle.

[16]   Apply tape to inside of article and bring a long-enough piece of it out over the edge to secure the handle in place. Let the clay set and harden.

[17]   Now cream the remainder of the mix until it can be applied with a soft art brush.

[18]   Apply creamy cement to the mended area, and blend it to a smooth join with handle and surrounding surfaces.

[19]   Clean off excess before it hardens. This is extremely important, because once this mix is married to your article, it is almost impossible to remove.

[20]   Remove any rough edges with razor blade, and in a feathering-out motion, reblend cement with surrounding areas.

[21]   Rebalance in sandbox, and let set and harden approximately 24 hours.

[22]   When cement is dry and hard, remove with a razor blade any

excess film left by cement on surrounding surfaces. You can get film off, but thick, hard stone will be virtually impossible to remove. There are ways, of course; you can use a hard rubber polishing disc in a handgrinder, or sandpaper. Sandpaper, however, is apt to scratch surrounding surfaces and do additional glaze damage.

[23]   Prepare Epoxyglass porcelainizing mix and blend in oil color to match article. Porcelainize mended surfaces.

[24]   Smooth until all edges and mends, as well as materials, are blended in with the body of the article.

[25]   Set aside to dry for 24 to 36 hours.

[26]   Decorate with oil paints and New Gloss Glaze.

[27]   Finish glazing with New Gloss Glaze.

[28]   Now, if you have to make a handle, be sure to read the section on handles in Chapter 2. You mold it out of Epoxybond Resin Putty and Hardener—make a pattern of a figure "5." Cut the pattern from paper. Fit it to your teapot. Try it on for size, as they say.

[29]   When satisfied it is appropriate, mold and duplicate your pattern for the teapot handle out of Epoxybond Resin Putty and Hardener mix.

[30]   When hard, wire-wind it and cream, and add a covering coat of the mix.

[31]   Drill holes in the ends of the handle approximately 1/2 inch deep. (Drills may be purchased with a hand grinder as part of the standard equipment.)

[32]   Drill holes in the top and bottom nubs where the handle attaches to the pot.

[33]   Insert dowels (use victrola needles—they do a very good job as pegs). Or, if you prefer, make holes through the nub ends of your pot, and push the wire ends through. Bend and press these ends down firmly in opposite directions to each other.

[34]   Tape the handle in place and cement, pushing the cement putty mix into the dowel holes. Cover the bent ends in the interior, and conceal all signs of the mend on the exterior with a creamy mix of the Epoxybond Resin Putty and Hardener. You must porcelainize the cement when it has hardened.

[35]   Set aside to harden. When hard, proceed as given in steps 22 through 27.

how to mend a
stoneware tureen

Examine this tureen after mending, and you will see it is a multipiece item, having a cover with a finial or ornamental handle at the top of the arch of the lid. Each piece has involved a separate mending job and should be reexamined to make sure mends are invisible.

A brief look at a tureen will reveal that it is a multipiece item. It will have a cover. The cover will have a finial, and the cover and finial will have to be properly reseated when mended to fit the tureen.

statement of the problem

The tureen itself will have finger handles or hand knobs, and it may also have a base, or a base and separate underpiece. If the underpiece is lacking, the tureen cover will undoubtedly provide a place or hole for the handle of the ladle to fit and go through so that the bowl of the ladle can set down in the bottom of the tureen.

To sum up, we may have multiple breakage and damage to the cover, the finial, the ladle, the handles, the base pieces, and the tureen itself.

step-by-step sequence

[1]   Inspect damaged pieces for broken cover, finial, ladle, base cracks, and chips. These will have to be repaired in accordance with procedures for same given under their respective headings in Chapter 2.

[2]   If the tureen is broken into more than three pieces, you will have to decide on its value to you. As far as mending it is concerned, unless it is an heirloom or wedding present, the time and good

materials it will take to restore it may not be worthwhile. A careful inspection will help you decide.

[3]   Plan assembly of the broken pieces.

[4]   Prepare strips of masking tape in lengths needed to secure the pieces to be fitted into the article.

[5]   Prepare Porcelainate cement. Mix powder and hardener on two-to-one basis.

[6]   Cement pieces into place in the article, secure with strips of masking tape from both the inside and the outside as needed, and set aside to dry and harden.

[7]   Examine for uneven edges and displacement. The thickness of the material you use will determine the amount of displacement. If the pieces do not fit together perfectly, wait until cement has hardened, and grind off unevenness before removing masking tape.

[8]   After grinding away ragged edges, reexamine for chips.

[9]   Remove tapes.

[10]   If you have chips, you should use Porcelainate mix to fill them in, removing all excess.

[11]   Place in sandbox to dry and harden.

[12]   Sand smooth any remaining rough edges.

[13]   If you have to put on a broken handle, cement the pieces together with Epoxybond Resin Putty and Hardener. Mix in equal parts. Let harden.

[14]   Grind a grid in the nubs of the handle (or finial), and grind grooves in ends of the handle (or finial). You can put in a cross shape ("X") or a single groove.

[15]   The base cement should be firm. Press the cement into the grooves of the nubs and into the handle (or finial).

[16]   Apply tape to inside of item and bring a long-enough piece of it out over the edge to secure the handle in place.

[17]   Now cream the remainder of the cement mix until it can be applied with a soft art brush.

[18]   Apply creamy cement to the mended area, and blend it to a smooth join with handle and surrounding surfaces.

[19]   Clean off excess. This is extremely important, because this clay cement mix will harden into a stone-hard substance, and once married to your article, is almost impossible to remove.

[20] Remove any rough edges with a razor blade, and in a feathering-out motion, reblend cement with surrounding areas.

[21] Rebalance in sandbox, and let set and harden for approximately 24 hours.

[22] When cement is beginning to dry and harden, remove with a razor blade any excess film left by cement on surrounding surfaces. You can get film off. Thick, hard stone will be virtually impossible to remove. There are ways, of course; you can use a hard rubber polishing disc in a hand grinder, or sandpaper. Sandpaper, however, is apt to scratch surrounding surfaces and do additional glaze damage.

[23] Prepare epoxy porcelainizing mix, and blend in oil color to match article. Porcelainize mended surfaces.

[24] Smooth until all edges and mends, as well as materials, are blended in with the body of the article.

[25] Set aside to dry for 24 to 36 hours.

[26] Decorate with oil paints tinted with New Gloss Glaze.

[27] Finish glazing with New Gloss Glaze (System 5).

how to mend faience, majolica, and soft paste pottery articles

Items made as soft paste pottery are not combined with the superior clay used to make stoneware. This does not mean that pottery pieces are inferior. Pottery is one of man's oldest crafts, and some of it is produced with incomparably beautiful deep glazes, designs, and colors. Almost all such pieces are ovenproof, chip resistant, and safe for cleaning in a dishwasher.

Some pottery is more porous than other kinds of earthenware and also far more provincial in feeling and charm. Most pottery pieces are natural for kitchens with a brick or tile floor and for the "early American" modern living-room decor.

There are many ornamental and decorative articles of pottery such as redware (or slip as it is also called), which is covered with brown or black glaze. Most of the German, Spanish, and Italian pottery is of this rich red with a luster pigment of a rich, iridescent, brown color. Red brick clay is predominant in pottery ware. And when red lead was added to the fluid clay for the rich shade it produced, the ware became thick, soft, and easily broken.

About 1900, gray, salt-glazed types of jugs and crocks were made, and by adding ground flint, the ware gained a flint-like hardness.

Among some of the most famous and perhaps the most familiar potteries are these famous names: Bennington, Lambeth, Delft, Leeds, Wedgwood, Sgraffito Ware, Majolica, Pennsylvania Slipware, and many others.

It must be mentioned in connection with mending that pottery differs from any other ware due to the density of the clay paste with which it is made. Therefore, the materials needed to mend it must be varied to meet the porosity of the article. Bear in mind that you can mend any article with System 2, but you may not find this system amenable to all articles. Therefore, try System 1 or 3—they may be more suitable for full restoration.

how to mend a pottery teapot

step-by-step sequence

[1]   Inspect damaged pieces for broken spout, handle, lip, finial, or cracks and chips. These will have to be repaired in accordance with procedures for same given under respective headings in Chapter 2.

[2]   Plan assembly of the two or three broken pieces.

[3]   Prepare strips of masking tape in lengths needed to secure the pieces to be fitted into the teapot.

[4]   Prepare cement mix in equal parts.

[5]   Cement pieces into place in the teapot, secure with strips of masking tape from both the inside and the outside, and set aside to dry and harden.

[6]   Examine for uneven edges and displacement. The thickness of the material you use will determine the amount of displacement. If the pieces do not fit together perfectly, wait until cement has hardened, and grind off unevenness before removing masking tape.

[7]   After grinding away ragged edges, reexamine for chips.

[8]   Remove tapes.

[9] If you have chips, you should use System 3 mix to fill the chips in, removing all excess cement.

[10] Place in sandbox to dry and harden.

[11] Sand any remaining rough edges until smooth.

[12] If you have to put on a broken spout or handle, cement the pieces together, and set aside to harden.

[13] Grind a grid in the top and bottom nubs on the teapot, and grind grooves in the top and bottom of the handle or spout. Grooves should be in the shape of an "**X**" and about 1/4 inch deep. (See Chapter 2 for additional data.)

[14] The base cement should be firm. Press the cement into the grooves and into the nubs.

[15] Apply tape to inside of the teapot, and bring a long-enough piece of it out over the top to secure the handle. If you are cementing a spout, use only enough of a piece of tape to support at vital points. Place a ball of Mortite between spout and body of the teapot to keep the spout at the right angle.

[16] Now cream the remainder of the cement until it can be applied with a soft art brush. Blend to a smooth join with all surrounding surfaces.

[17] Apply a finishing coat of creamed cement.

[18] Clean off excess, and set aside to harden.

[19] Remove any rough edges with razor blade while cement is firm but not hard, and again feather-out and reblend cement.

[20] Rebalance in sandbox, and let set and harden for approximately 24 hours.

[21] When cement is dry and hard, remove with a razor blade any excess film left by cement on surrounding surfaces. You can get film off. Thick, hard stone will be virtually impossible to remove. There are ways, of course; you can use a hard rubber polishing disc in a handgrinder, or sandpaper. Sandpaper, however, is apt to scratch surrounding surfaces and do additional glaze damage.

[22] Prepare epoxy porcelainizing mix, and blend in oil color to match the teapot. Porcelainize mended surfaces.

[23] Smooth until all edges and mends, as well as materials, are blended in with the body of the teapot.

[24] Set aside to dry for 24 to 36 hours.

[25] Decorate with oil paints and mix with New Gloss Glaze.

[26] Finish glazing with New Gloss Glaze (System 5).

how to mend majolica

step-by-step sequence

[1]   Inspect damaged pieces for broken spout, handle, or cracks and chips. These will have to be repaired in accordance with procedures for same given under their respective headings in Chapter 2.

[2]   If your article has a broken handle and is chipped, cracked, and broken into more than three pieces, it may not be worth your time and the good materials it will take to restore it. A careful inspection will help you decide.

[3]   Plan assembly of the broken pieces.

[4]   Prepare strips of masking tape in lengths needed to secure the pieces to be fitted into the article.

[5]   Prepare cement mix in equal parts.

[6]   Cement pieces into place in the article, secure with strips of masking tape from both the inside and the outside, and set aside to dry and harden.

[7]   Examine for uneven edges and displacement. The thickness of the material you use will determine the amount of displacement. If the pieces do not fit together perfectly, wait until cement has hardened, and grind off unevenness before removing masking tape.

[8]   After grinding away ragged edges, reexamine for chips.

[9]   Remove tapes.

[10] If you have chips, you should use Porcelainate mix to fill the chips in, removing all excess.

[11] Place in sandbox or balance in a bed of wax to dry and harden.

[12] Sand any remaining rough edges until smooth, or add an additional coat of clay cement.

[13] If you have to put on a broken handle, cement the pieces together. Let harden.

[14] Grind a grid in the top and bottom nubs on the article, and grind grooves in top and bottom of handle. You can put in a cross shape ("**X**") or a single groove.

[15] The base cement should be firm. Press the cement into the grooves of the article's nubs and into the handle.

[16]   Apply tape to inside of article, and bring a long-enough piece of it out over the edge to secure the handle in place.

[17]   Now cream the remainder of the mix until it can be applied with a soft art brush.

[18]   Apply creamy cement to the mended area, and blend it to a smooth join with handle and surrounding surfaces.

[19]   Clean off excess. This is extremely important, because this cement mix will harden into a stone-hard substance, and once married to your article, is almost impossible to remove.

[20]   Remove any rough edges with solvent and a razor blade, and in a feathering-out motion, reblend cement with surrounding areas.

[21]   Rebalance in wax bed or sandbox, and let set and harden for approximately 24 hours.

[22]   When cement is dry and hardened, remove with solvent and a razor blade any excess film left by cement on surrounding surfaces. You can get film off. Thick, hard stone will be virtually impossible to remove. There are ways, of course; you can use a hard rubber polishing wheel in a handgrinder. Sandpaper is apt to scratch surrounding surfaces and do additional glaze damage.

[23]   Prepare Epoxyglass porcelainizing mix, and blend in oil color to match article. Porcelainize mended surfaces.

[24]   Smooth until all edges and mends, as well as materials, are blended in with the body of the article.

[25]   Set aside to dry for 24 to 36 hours.

[26]   Decorate with oil paints and New Gloss Glaze.

[27]   Finish glazing with New Gloss Glaze.

how to mend slipware

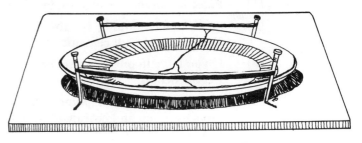

Broken pieces cemented and clamped together are held tightly
by nailed rubber band fasteners. The rubber bands pull
the pieces together tighter as the tension is increased.

step-by-step sequence

[1]   Inspect damaged pieces for broken spout, handle, or cracks and chips. These will have to be repaired in accordance with procedures given under their respective headings in Chapter 2.

[2]   If your article has a broken handle and is chipped, cracked, and broken into more than three pieces, it may not be worth your time and the good materials it will take to restore it. A careful inspection will help you decide.

[3]   Plan assembly of the broken pieces.

[4]   Prepare strips of masking tape in lengths needed to secure the pieces to be fitted into the article.

[5]   Prepare cement mix using System 3 in equal parts.

[6]   Cement pieces into place in the article, secure with masking tape from the inside and outside, and set aside to dry and harden.

[7]   Examine for uneven edges and displacement. The thickness of the material you use will determine the amount of displacement. If the pieces do not fit together perfectly, wait until cement has hardened, and grind off unevenness before removing masking tape.

[8]   After grinding away ragged edges, reexamine for chips.

[9]   Remove tapes.

[10]   If you have chips, you should use the resin putty cement mix to fill the chips in, removing all excess.

[11]   Place in sandbox, or balance in a bed of wax to dry and harden.

[12]   Sand any remaining rough edges until smooth.

[13]   If you have to put on a broken handle, cement the pieces together. Let harden.

[14]   Grind a grid in the top and bottom nubs of the article, and grind grooves in top and bottom of handle. You can put in a cross shape ("X") or a single groove.

[15]   The base cement should be firm. Press the cement into the grooves of the article's nubs and into the handle.

[16]   Apply tape to inside of article, and bring a long-enough piece of it out over the edge to secure the handle in place.

[17]   Now cream the remainder of the mix until it can be applied with a soft art brush.

[18]   Apply creamy cement to the mended area, and blend it to a smooth join with handle and surrounding surfaces.

[19]   **Clean off excess. This is extremely important, because this cement mix will harden into a stone-hard substance, and once married to your article, is almost impossible to remove.**

[20]   **Remove any rough edges with razor blade, and in a feathering-out motion, reblend cement with surrounding areas.**

[21]   **Rebalance in wax bed or sandbox, and let set and harden for approximately 24 hours.**

[22]   **When cement is dry and hard, remove with a razor blade any excess film left by cement on surrounding surfaces. You can get film off. Thick, hard stone will be virtually impossible to remove. There are ways, of course; you can use a hard rubber polishing wheel in a hand grinder. Sandpaper is apt to scratch surrounding surfaces and do additional glaze damage.**

[23]   **Prepare Epoxyglass porcelainizing mix, and blend in oil color to match article. Porcelainize mended surfaces.**

[24]   **Smooth until all edges and mends, as well as materials, are blended in with the body of the article.**

[25]   **Set aside to dry for 24 to 36 hours.**

[26]   **Decorate with oil paints and mix with New Gloss Glaze.**

[27]   **Finish glazing with New Gloss Glaze (System 5).**

how to mend alabaster, marble, and soapstone

step-by-step sequence

[1]   **Study the break and the grain of the marble or alabaster. Clean the broken surfaces thoroughly with a solution of Soilax.**

[2]   **You may have a problem with balance, say an arm is broken off a statue. Sand, of course, is the answer plus whatever taping or other structuring materials you may need to support the broken part while the mending material is hardening.***

[3]   **Use a hand grinder to cut a grid or drill out holes for dowels. All edges must be fitted together, so be careful not to spoil the edges.**

[4]   **Make a firm paste of Porcelainate Powder and Hardener.**

*Alabaster is very similar to marble, but it is much more transparent. However, you may mend it with the same materials or make a mix of plaster and beeswax.

[5]   Have sand and tapes or clamps ready to apply immediately after cementing.

[6]   Color Porcelainate mix. Do not blend the color in evenly. Stir it in so that it will have veins of color to match the marble or alabaster.

[7]   Let the mend set up, and recement surface.

[8]   Doweling, if needed, is of course set into the marble first, cemented, and hardened. The filler is cemented in around the dowels.

[9]   Melted liquid wax or beeswax is used to completely conceal the mend. The advantage lies in the soft marblelike finish such wax gives finished marble work.

A material useful in mending soapstone is as follows:

[1]   Make a mix of Epoxyglass Resin and Epoxyglass Hardener. Allow it to set for a few minutes until it thickens.

[2]   When mix is beginning to thread (as in making candy), apply firmly with stiff brush or spatula, working quickly. Keep this material off hands.

[3]   Clamp mend, or tape. Have any pieces of tape precut.

[4]   Let cement set.

[5]   Cut away excess with a razor blade. Be careful not to scratch or leave scrape marks on surface.

[6]   Finish restoration with a mixture of melted beeswax and carnauba. This mixture will match alabaster perfectly.

[7]   Mix one part carnauba wax to two parts beeswax. Beeswax comes in several grades of color from white to dark brown, so the mix can be the shade you need to match.

how to mend ivory

This ivory monkey holding a melon snuff bottle with a jade stopper was simply restored with Epoxyglass Resin and Hardener combined with Epoxybond White Finishing Paste colored to match the ivory shade of these bottles.

Above are two ivory snuff bottles restored with a
simple application of Epoxyglass Resin and Hardener
combined with Epoxybond White Finishing Pasted colored
to match the ivory shade of these bottles.

step-by-step sequence

[1]   Restorations in ivory are difficult, requiring an almost professional skill. Clean article thoroughly.

[2]   Prepare wax mix and Epoxyglass Resin mix.

[3]   The Epoxyglass Resin mix should be used as cement.

[4]   Doweling is recommended if the mend involves parts to be joined.

[5]   Parts to be made may be molded with wax or plastic wood (see Missing Parts in Chapter 2). Or:

[6]   Use plastic wood, and fill in layer by layer.

[7]   Allow to set and harden in the mold or section to be filled.

[8]   If molded, remove when hard from mold, and cement into place with Epoxyglass Resin and Epoxyglass Hardener mix.

[9]   Sand with very fine grain paper.

[10]   Rub with liquid wax to smooth finish, colored to suit, using tempera or watercolor in wax mix to blend.

how to mend or simulate jade or other hard colored stones

step-by-step sequence

[1]   Prepare mix of Epoxyglass Resin and Epoxyglass Hardener, equal parts.

[2]   Color with Grumbacher's oil paint. Squeeze right out of the tube, and mix into epoxy carefully until right shade is obtained to match the jade, ruby, or other hard stone.

[3]   If you are replacing a missing stone by simulation, follow molding procedure for restoring a missing part (Chapter 2), and make a rubber mold of a similar stone.

[4]   Pour mix into mold, and let set and harden.

[5]   When hard, cement into place.

[6]   Glaze.

Note: If you have broken metal parts, see your jeweler about resoldering. The rest you can mend yourself.

how to mend lacquerware

The mending of lacquerware is usually professional. It is almost a lost art. However, you can do it.

step-by-step sequence

[1]   You will need clear liquid New Gloss Glaze (boilproof).

[2]   Fill in the cracks and chips with clear lacquer. Color to shade desired.

[3]   Use several thin coats until built up to surface.

[4]   Let each layer harden. Use the fingernail test coat until surfaces are equal.

[5] Use fine sable brush to paint in a design to match surrounding motifs.

[6] Color from the oil tubes is mixed with the liquid glaze to desired shades.

[7] Mix the various shades you need, as you need them. Do not mix the shades before you need them, because the glaze quickly dries.

how to mend antique chalkware articles

Colored chalkware.

step-by-step sequence

[1] Replace broken parts with plaster.

[2] Do *not* use "Plaster of Paris."

[3] Missing parts can be cast in rubber molds, as described in the section about missing parts in Chapter 2.

[4] If you need only a small quantity of plaster, you may obtain the type used by dental supply houses.

[5] Working with plaster, you will want to have a pan of water handy.

[6] Smooth away excess with dampened fingers.

[7] To simulate the Pennsylvania Dutch colors and decorations common to chalkware, you may find some guides, ideas, and studies in Peter Hunt books at any library.

[8]   **You will be using tempera or watercolors, not oil paints.**

[9]   **Decorate in accordance with the motif or design original to the piece, and let your imagination be your guide.**

decorating china, glass, and pottery

restoring a decoration

You have learned the fundamentals of how to mend and the basic procedures of repair and restoration. You have even learned how to recreate porcelain and conceal the lines showing where the article was broken. Now that you have learned to remold and reform your broken article back into a whole piece, are you ready to decorate it? Maybe, or almost, but not quite!

It is precisely at this point that many china menders stop. Perhaps you have assumed that once the basic sequences were mastered, redecorating your mended article would automatically fall into place. China painting is a field in itself and is a challenge to talented ceramists, let alone someone who has just learned the basic techniques of how to mend china and glass. So what shall we do to decorate our mended treasure?

A poorly decorated article can detract from the beauty, usefulness, and value of the piece, regardless of the pains you have taken to mend it beautifully. Whatever you do to redecorate the piece now can bring it to life or ruin it. For example, suppose you mended a beautiful bowl-shaped, porcelain flowerpot. Let us assume it was broken and mended as shown in the illustration on pages 37–38.

The drawings clearly show the line of the breaks. Fortunately, the piece broke along the strain of the bowl in both sides— nice, clean lines. Also, the flower decorations are in Chinese mandarin orange and gold against the plain white background of the porcelain. It is a beautiful piece, but the breaks still show and need redecorating in order to conceal the mend.

decorate to fit the style of the piece

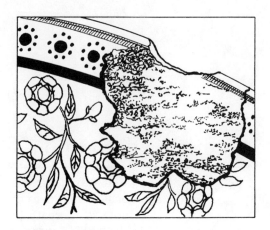

Before the mend.

After the mend.

Redecoration.

When planning any decoration, study the size, shape, and character (style and design) of the piece.

In the piece we are considering, you should be able to draw additional floral decorations to harmonize with those on each panel. In this case, you will paint your ascending vine of stems and leaves in a movement that takes them right up the lines of the breaks on both sides. Accustom yourself to thinking in terms of the piece to be redecorated, and you will automatically reject unsuitable motifs and decorations Do not think of your decoration to conceal a mend as a thing apart. Make it an integral part of the article, even though it was never there to begin with.

When you are faced with concealing rim chip mends, borders of almost any kind can be elaborated or be made more effective. You can use stripes on a tall vase that lends itself to such a motif. The owner may be startled but pleased, because the decoration will become an integral part of the piece.

An article such as a Kutani plate or vase lends itself beautifully to small all-over gold patterns. You may easily learn to copy stars, leaf molds, floral sprays, wavy lines and gold leading.

choose your own
decorating technique

In more than one instance, you may lightly lacquer the area to be decorated. Then, after the lacquer is dry, take onion paper, trace the design in heavy pencil, and Scotch-tape sheets of gold leaf to the reverse side of the paper under the design. Then tape the paper to the area to be decorated, and using a hard lead pencil, retrace your design. Upon removing the paper, the gold lead decoration will remain, adding lustre and beauty to the entire area and providing perfect camouflage for the mend.

color

Your choice of color must be in accord with the article mended. Also, in coloring any decoration, keep your application and color range simple, as well as toned down. The fewer and softer your colors, the easier it will be to execute the decoration, and the design will be more pleasing to live with over a period of time. Shading your basic colors is quite acceptable.

You will do well to keep in mind that colors are either warm or cold to the eye. Red, yellow, brown, and all cousins of those colors are warm, while, blue, and green are on the cold side of the color spectrum. Try to keep away from using bright yellow. You will have better results using other shades of warm colors, such as the reds and brown, for large areas of decoration. Red is better used as an accent color. In combining in floral patterns, use the blue-greens, gray-blues, and pastel shades. Adding a bit of brown to your blues or greens will soften them and give depth and richness of tone. Don't be afraid of mistakes.

If your brush slips or a smudge occurs, dip cheesecloth or brush in acetone, and with several quick, light strokes remove, then relacquer and redecorate.

Color applied by brush will show as a raised effect on the surface of your article. Your color application will be a mix of lacquer or glaze. If the raised effect is disturbing to the overall appearance, let your colors dry. You may heat-dry using an oven set at about 150 degrees for an hour or two.

Sand with 6/0 or the finest sandpaper you can buy until even with surrounding surfaces. Now apply glaze. If your article has been mended with china clay or fine white powder cement, you may spray glaze with a coat or two of Kemkote clear glaze.

Be careful to use a glaze that matches the gloss of the article. You may want a satin finish (Blair's clear satin finish glaze) or a matte.

On bisque or eggshell finish articles, no glaze or finishing coat is required. The color mix, although made with glossy glaze or lacquer, will blend out to complete smoothness when dried and lightly sanded.

working with an airbrush

I have not listed an airbrush for nonprofessional work. However, for many types of repairing, colors (or white porcelainizing) can very well be applied with an airbrush. The well known F-2 or the HS-5 with the "D" type compressor, or equal, are well-suited to airbrush work. You will find that you have to adjust the nozzle to modify color for decorating china or glass. Also, you may want to have or to get a tank of compressed air to use instead of a noisy air compressor. Tanks come in 5-lb. or 10-lb. sizes, equipped with the proper airbrush hose connection. No problem, but it takes skill and practice to learn how to airbrush china repairs with success.

Color must be mixed to exactly the right consistency. The spray nozzle has to undergo adjustments for china decoration spraying. Proper distance from the article to be sprayed must be considered, as well as covering up areas you do not want to decorate.

Through practice you learn. It is a skill that grows, not one you can acquire by following strict rules of procedure, as on mending.

finishes

There are many kinds of finishes used in decorating glass and china, and still others for pottery. The types commonly used are: High gloss or frosted finish glaze on glass; dull glaze for parian or bisque articles; opaque or porcelainized glaze on porcelain (china); and clear glaze, satin-finish matte, or flat on pottery or earthenware.

Glazing to a ceramist has an entirely different meaning than it does to you. The finishes mentioned above have a variety of applications and uses.

use of color on china

Colors may be mixed with various mediums or systems. You may premix colors with the Porcelainate to match the areas you intend to mend, or you may be concerned with concealing mended areas and filling in or redecorating damaged patterns.

Colors should be added into the mixing medium. Use a spatula to blend the color to the shade desired. Avoid using an art brush until the mix is perfected. Brushes are for painting and are quickly ruined if used to mix colors with mixing mediums (systems).

Colors should be mixed on an absolutely clean tile, square of heavy white paper, or palette free of dust.

Study the area to be redecorated. Familiarize yourself with the design. Get the *feel* of it.

color matching

Almost anyone will learn by experience how to match colors. White epoxy finishing paste may be used for white tints. To obtain tints, you may wish to add to this basic set of colors. Various shades and tints in artist's oil paints are available in every craft shop and in many hardware and department stores. China painters may use their basic powders and oil color paints in ready-to-use form.

Flesh tint is suitable for porcelain cheeks on figurines. It may be toned.

Leaves, stems, foliage, and vegetation vary between a shaded green and greenish yellow. The tint or shade desired can be obtained by mixing viridian or dark earth green with yellow ochre. Of course, if you do not have these additional tubes of color on hand, mix blue, white, and yellow until you reach the color you want.

bright colors

Bright colors may be made dull by adding Payne's gray or a touch of burnt sienna. China Trade Porcelain may be matched by toning white with these latter colors until the blue-gray of that ware is matched.

crackle effects on china

You may also recreate the crackle effect on oriental ware by scratching the mended surface with the point of a needle and rubbing Vandyck brown into the scratch marks. You may do well to trace the crackle design first with a well-sharpened hard pencil.

unusual glazes

In mending bisque, which is unglazed porcelain, you will have to create, as well as duplicate, the white unglazed finish or the color found on such bisque pieces as jasperware. In reproducing a handle on a Wedgwood sugar bowl, it is necessary to blend ultramarine with red to produce a strong violet blue, which matches the Wedgwood color. Once the right shape of handle is obtained, the color can be blended into the Epoxybond Adhesive Putty mix, System 3. Once blended in the color is always there and the handle when shaped and rubbed down will have the stonelike unglazed finish of bisque.

ivory as a color

Epoxybond Adhesive Putty, System 3, may be colored with yellow ochre to match ivory. How to use the epoxy putty to repair ivory is described in Chapter 5.

mother-of-pearl finishes

There are many examples of iridescent china such as the tea and table services labeled Noritake and Nippon. Irish Belleek china also has a glaze closely resembling mother-of-pearl. Mother-of-pearl nail polish or varnish may serve your purpose in obtaining a match or a satisfactory blend.

mixing colors with kaolin

Mixing colors (whether precompounded or in powder form), Kaolin, and the epoxy resins of Systems 2 and 3 can be used.

When epoxy resin is compounded with Kaolin, System 3, you have a moldable epoxy putty. Any color can be mixed with this putty. Should you desire to increase the whiteness of the basic putty, add titanium oxide. Titanium oxide is *true* white and is basic to all white paint. Titanium will make the epoxy putty sticky. However, you may keep your fingers fairly free of it by dipping them in alcohol or methylated spirit, either of which is easily obtainable from a hardware shop or drugstore.

dull colors

white as a finish

White is probably the most difficult of all colors to match. It would be well for you to attempt it in daylight only. White varies in a broad spectrum of shades and tints. For example, Chinese porcelains are usually gray-blue or gray with a hint of pink or blue-green. The glaze and the color of the article are one, because true porcelain is fired as a body with the glaze on it. Many of the China Trade Porcelains were glazed with yellow ochre.

White glazes are not necessarily white or dull. To match yellow ochre glaze, use Flake White oil paint (Grumbacher's or equal), and mix it with ordinary picture varnish or shellac. This mixture can then be mixed with yellow ochre or any other color to produce the exact shade of the glaze required. To dull the glaze, add white spirit, which is sold commercially in spray cans labeled glass frosting. Use sparingly!

Other shades of white may be obtained by adding cans of car touch-up paint to your supplies. A slight amount sprayed onto your palette and mixed into the Porcelainate or Epoxybond Resins of System 2 can produce the exact shade of color required.

white bisque or parian ware

White bisque or parian ware does not have a glaze. Even so, the covering white finish though dull has an unusual sheen. Almost unmatchable. It is possible to obtain Kaolin from a clay products company. Make a paste or slip of this material and blend it with System 1. You may also blend precolored white plaster into the mix until you have exactly the right shade and texture required for application.

gold finishes on china

Gold finishing is done with powdered gold or gold leaf.

step-by-step sequence

[1]   Make a simple outline, if necessary, using a light crayon or art pencil on the area to be outlined. You may find this necessary for the lid of a box, the rim of a plate, or the handle of a cup or pot.

[2]   The outline should be applied freehand.

[3]   If you must trace a design or fill in over mended areas, copy or trace the design by overlaying it with thin onionskin tracing paper.

[4]   Fill in the missing areas of the design on the paper.

[5]   Transfer the design. This is done by attaching a piece of carbon paper to the reverse or underside of the onionskin paper.

[6]   If you have traced the design with a good sharp black pencil, go over the black lines carefully when transferring. Assure that you have not omitted any part of the original design.

[7]   The lines of the pattern design should be clearly transferred. If they are not, secure tracing paper to the article with clear tape and go over it again.

[8]   Once you are satisfied that the design has been transferred, prepare the gold powder by mixing it with New Gloss Glaze a drop or two at a time.

[9]   Sketch in the gold patterns with this liquid gold.

[10]   Let dry.

decorating china

You may be a left-handed baseball pitcher, but you can still draw a leaf, a stem, or a flower. Anyone who can write his name can do it. There are some who can paint and draw who can *not* write! You can do it.

backgrounding

step-by-step sequence

[1] With an acrylic brush flat and lightly spread, dip into the pre-mixed color medium. Wipe off any excess.

[2] With a "C" stroke, shade in the paint so that it is heavy to one side and light on the other.

[3] Stroke in the shading, backgrounding your outline.

[4] In reaching a high line, draw your brush lightly and quickly down toward yourself.

[5] Same on circling lines. Start at the top and come down toward yourself. This will give you steady control over the resulting line, shading and effect the backgrounding desired.

[6] When you have put in the background with outlining, paint the area by applying the color mix thinly and smoothly.

[7] Let the outline dry and harden before starting to paint on the finish coat.

[8] Then add each premix of color necessary to complete the overall designed pattern.

[9] Each color to be added must be shaded into the individual area of the pattern and then it must be blended to match the existing pattern.

[10] Always keep the background color darker at the base of a leaf, stem petal, or at the base outer edge of any design.

covering over mended areas

In covering over mended areas where broken lines still show background, colors may be shaded over with contrasts between the colors considered necessary to use.

Red and yellow are considered china painters' colors. They are also sunshine colors. Yellow-green is still a warm color —green is cool. Violet approaches a neutral. Blue is a cold color. Violet-blue is cool. A pale yellow color shaded with pink or red, or yellow red around a blue pattern will provide contrast and distract attention from a broken line. Shading colors to a depth to provide contrast must not be definite. Any color placed next to a sharply contrasting color will intensify both—glazing will soften the colors you use as it absorbs the intensity.

iridescent effects in china painting

These effects are achieved by applying darker colors over lighter colors. Try mother-of-pearl nail polish!

step-by-step sequence

[1]   **Lightly glaze the area to be painted.**

[2]   **Premix the lightest shade of the color to be used.**

[3]   **Apply over the glaze.**

[4]   **Let it dry and harden.**

[5]   **Following your preestablished outline or backgrounding, apply the darker color, then the lighter color. Shade it in. If a brush does not do the job, try a small atomizer. Thin the mix with acetone or alcohol. Keep the nozzle clean and free of excess. Test as you mix!**

[6]   **Let harden and glaze.**

[7]   **Using an extremely fine sable art brush, apply any veining necessary to the design or pattern.**

[8]   **Apply final glaze coat when paint has dried.**

a high-gloss finish

A high-gloss finish should be applied by hand brush, because it dries too quickly for air-brush application.

In applying a high-gloss finish, carefully examine your article. The kind of material you have used to repair can be puckered, drawn, and ruined by a high-gloss varnish spray. Acrylic high-gloss spray can ruin your entire repair because of its fast-drying properties. Any oil colors or unprotected epoxy mending material it touches can be drawn, cracked, buckled, expanded, and contracted until it is totally ruined.

Also, if you use a spray gloss such as Blair's, don't press your luck beyond one coat. A second coat may react with undesirable crackling and splitting in the glaze and ruin the appearance of your decoration and mend.

This is not to say that you cannot use high-gloss glaze. Some items, as well as some materials, such as Royal Copenhagen

Christmas Plates, that you have mended with white cement powder, can be finished with high-gloss spray after color has been applied, heat-dried, and sanded.

New Gloss Glaze can give beautiful results. When it is too thick, thin it out before use with lacquer thinner (methylate type or acetone).

Dull glaze is achieved with a pigment or plaster. This produces an almost flat finish. However, parian or bisque has a lovely eggshell glow that cannot seriously be called flat. Color should be added in a ratio of ten to one in order to obtain the color match you require, because this type of dull finish seriously affects color. In good natural light you will have no trouble achieving the shade desired.

clear transparent glaze finish

Clear transparent glaze finish is used on all kinds of wares including glass. The glaze may have a soft finish, or it may be extremely matte. Somewhere in between you may want to make your clear glaze a satiny or frosted compromise.

To make a matte finish you may use Blair's or equal matte glaze spray, or you may prefer to add zinc oxide. Small quantities may be bought from your pharmacist. The ratio of oxide to the lacquer should start at about one part oxide to ten parts lacquer. Do not exceed one to three or you will have no sheen at all.

colored glazing

It is easy to use glaze, lacquer, or New Gloss Glaze as a base to obtain any finish you want, including that of producing colored, transparent, glaze finishes, by adding oxides, stains, or oil colors from tubes of artist colors. Of course, you will have to do a little experimenting to find the exact shade of color desired to match your article. Color and stains may be added in liquid or dry form. Check with your local art supply dealer for a list of the many stains and colors available. Buy basic colors and add others as you need them.

redecorating glass

Redecorating glass requires patience and care. The redecoration may require enameling, frosting, or preparation to duplicate, as nearly as possible, the once smooth, flawless surface of clear crystal.

In each case the preparation must proceed with care. Since decorating or painting in a design or pattern on clear crystal is the most difficult, let us explore this problem first.

The techniques for redecorating glass are not different from those used to paint an article of chinaware, perhaps because the technique is the same, but the approach may vary in any given mending problem. After all, the problem in every case is to make the repair and then finish it so that it matches as closely as possible the surrounding surfaces of the article. Damage to clear glass complicates the problem of concealment.

Just about the same kinds of damage occur to glass as to china. They are classified as flake chips, rim or lip chips, missing parts, and multiple breaks. Glass does not suffer glaze damage as it is not glazed, but it is easily chipped—some glass articles have edges that are apt to suffer damage more quickly than china articles—and the base of a glass article usually needs greater care and protection from sudden shock.

Glass can withstand great pressure but a sudden blow, or shock from extreme change of temperature in air or water may cause damage.

Glass cannot be added to glass to make a repair; it would take molten glass to do it. Molten glass cannot be added to cool glass because of the shock of temperature change to both the hot and cold glass. Glass, like china, is made at high temperatures and cannot be subjected to heat again except very gradually.

how to use epoxy cement mix, system 3, to redecorate glass

There are various kinds of epoxy resin cements and resin cement hardeners that can be combined to form crystal clear forms, such as the beautiful, lucite paperweights we see in every gift shop, and other useful plastic menders for decorative clear-glass projects.

One of the leading oil refiners spent in excess of $20 million in research to develop highly sophisticated epoxies and resins that could be used in countless ways such as the fabrication of spacecraft, as well as for other industrial and commercial purposes. Glass can be successfully mended with such epoxy resin material.

Our purpose, of course, is to find a suitable epoxy cement

and hardener with which to mend glass. Such material would have to meet the mender's requirement that it harden quickly, join two pieces together so that they do not come apart, remain as nearly invisible as possible, substitute for a missing part and, in the final analysis, duplicate the glass article being mended.

Many companies make materials that answer one or more of these requirements, but only System 2 for glassmending, Epoxyglass Resin and Hardener, answers all of these specifications.

The material can be mixed in equal parts, and oil paints can be added to it for color. In addition, Epoxybond White Resin, System 4, Finishing Paste may be stirred in evenly with this epoxyglass resin cement mix, System 2, to produce a porcelainizing effect, such as you would need if you were mending a broken article of white milk glass.

There is an old saying: "It does not matter what you've got, it's what you do with it." You will soon agree completely with that statement in the use of epoxy cement and colors in painting. There are a variety of professional techniques, including those you have learned in this book for grinding anchor grooves, rivet grooves, footers, "X"s, and the whole array. However, you may lay this knowledge and skill aside in redecorating mended articles of glass. You may need a handgrinder and carbide rubber wheels for polishing; however, these are not recommended in the nonprofessional grinding into glass for mending, restoring, or in any procedure or preparation for redecorating glass.

You are now aware of the problems of delicate balancing that can arise in mending twisted candelabra arms, broken stemware, broken glass clowns, fingers, heads, bowls, ladles, hurricane shades, leaky liquor decanters, bottle stoppers, and hundreds of other gorgeous articles of glass. Some of these articles may be blown, others may be molded or freeform. However, you will rarely, if ever, have to grind to mend any of these articles in order to get the results needed to meet the owner's satisfaction.

Many early repairs may be based on the strict techniques taught in grinding. Do not abandon such techniques (habits, if you will), but reserve them for highly professional work, and other mending areas. They are not considered necessary in redecorating glass.

Mending articles such as lamps, candelabra, mirrors, and decorative accessories such as ashtrays, figurines, cigarette and jewelry boxes, toiletries and perfume bottles, are dealt with in Chapter 4.

The materials and equipment needed for mending cooking

and tableware glass is minimal. The skill required to redecorate and conceal the mend is emphasized instead. There are many reasons for this, not the least of which has to do with the mending problem. Glass is slick—so is the material with which you are going to mend. Glass can be badly out of balance when it is broken. You cannot use a sandbox easily—you must use care in placing the article in it.

You must use great care to prevent sand getting into the mend. It seems to have an affinity (how true) for glass, as well as for the epoxy. All such substances as clay, sand, epoxy, glass, and the like are plastic-like in nature, or become so under various conditions.

Another problem you may have while mending and re-decorating glass is whether you can remove lime deposit from old bottles. You can, if you wish to, use hydrofluoric acid. It can give you a dangerous *burn* if not used with extreme caution. It is the only chemical I know that will remove lime from so called "sick glass." It is obtainable from industrial chemists and wholesale supply houses. Use of hydrofluoride may have more than one re-sult. The second result is to slightly haze or frost the inside of your glass. Why? Because it dissolves glass. Not all glass is alike or made with the same substances. Good lead glass should come out clear and brilliant. A poor quality glass made with lime will immediately frost. In the first place, the better the quality of the glass, the less likely it is to get sick or show lime deposit.

You may use such products as *Rust-Out* and even the common steam-iron cleaner fluids to clean out "sick glass" de-canters and perfume bottles. These cleaners are relatively safe to use, because they will not burn your clothes or hands if inad-vertently splashed. *Be warned: Hydrofluoric acid will!*

step-by-step sequence

[1]   **Thoroughly clean the mended surfaces with alcohol or acetone.**

[2]   **Assemble colors. You may need:**
      white (Epoxybond White Finishing Paste)

flake white or	**brown**
titanium oxide	**umber**
black	**raw umber**
green	**purple**
yellow ochre	**ultramarine blue**
yellow	**crimson lake red**
orange	**other**
cobalt blue	

[3]   Give the mend or ground area of the mend a coat of System 3.

[4]   If you are going to use gold, apply a thin coat of venetian red *first*, because it will *set the gold* when applied and improve its gold leaf effect.

[5]   Use a flat glaze over the lines of the cracks or mended join.

[6]   Apply any design you have traced from a matching article or one you have preselected.

[7]   System 3 may be used to obtain the shaded color required by adding the selected colors.

[8]   Keep your decorating brush pointed and free of excess material.

[9]   As you apply color to an outlined leaf or flower, add a touch of white to lighten the tint. Always work the dark color from the base of the leaf stem or flower petal upward, outward, and away from the base toward the outer edge.

[10]   Oil color may be added to the clear epoxy mix, System 3. The color effect required may be achieved by mixing, by stirring, or by streaking.

[11]   Spread out the applied mix by design until the repair is completely concealed.

[12]   Lightly spray with New Gloss Glaze when design is dry and hard to the touch.

redecorating opaque glass (high-gloss finish)

step-by-step sequence

[1]   Prepare System 3.

[2]   Mix color with System 4 to the exact shade required.

[3]   Combine systems.

[4]   Prepare outline of design by using onionskin paper tracing applied to area to be decorated.

[5]   Apply color mix in thin coats.

[6]   When dry, add thin coats as required to match prior design, or blend to surrounding areas.

[7]   When decorated area has hardened, glaze with a finish coat of New Gloss Glaze.

decorating clear frosted glass (satin finish)

Clear or frosted glass may be recognized as camphor glass, coin glass, or by many other generic terms given to it.

step-by-step sequence

[1] Prepare System 3.

[2] Apply the mixture to the mended areas.

[3] Set aside to harden.

[4] Lightly spray or brush on "white spirit" or glass frosting (available at hardware and art supply stores).

[5] Add thin coats as required to blend or match frosted areas.

redecorating pottery (plain)

step-by-step sequence

[1] Prepare color mix and blend with System 3.

[2] Cream the mixture to a slurry that matches the areas surrounding the mend.

[3] Apply the creamy mix or slurry to the mended area, and blend it to a smooth join with the surrounding areas.

[4] Permit this first coat to dry and harden.

[5] Sand away any excess.

[6] Reapply thin coats one at a time until a perfect blend is obtained.

redecorating pottery (designed with floral or other art patterns)

It would be well to read the entire section on redecorating chinaware before proceeding with an article such as Mason's colored ironstone or a salt-glazed stein. There is much to review in redecorating china regarding colors and the mixtures you can obtain with them. Also, in the pottery field, there are many kinds of glazes, as well as unglazed articles. Slipware and majolica are highly decorated and color mixtures with glaze are essential to the craft of redecorating these varieties of pottery.

Any of these articles may be decorated with oil paints and Systems 2, 3, or 4. These may be varied by the use or addition of glass frosting on unglazed wares; it would be well for you to study use of white spirit and/or glass frosting prior to application.

step-by-step sequence

[1] **Prepare the design by draft, transfer, or stencil.**

[2] **Prepare System 3 as a slurry.**

[3] **Prepare color mix from powdered colors.**

[4] **Combine to the shade required. You now have a mix that can be applied to *unglazed* earthenware.**

[5] **Apply to the design with an acrylic brush.**

[6] **Permit first coat to dry.**

[7] **Apply additional coats as required.**

[8] **Reblend to match surrounding areas.**

[9] **Permit to set and harden.**

[10] **If you are decorating slipware or majolica, prepare System 4 with color mix.**

[11] **Paint in design over mended surfaces.**

[12] **If design already exists and is mutilated by the mend or repair, paint in to restore the design.**

[13] **If the mended area goes beyond the design, *extend the design* to cover as required.**

[14] **Add final cover coats as needed. Do not glaze unless necessary.**

special techniques for special finishes

gold leaf, silver leaf, and other metallic effects

To achieve a gold leaf effect on porcelain (china), you will use Systems 2 and 4.

step-by-step sequence

[1]   **Mix a small quantity of Epoxyglass Resin and Hardener with Epoxybond Resin White Finishing Paste.**

[2]   **Let this begin to thicken.**

[3]   **Apply when stringy.**

[4]   **Dip an art brush into the metallic powder, and very lightly brush onto the surface of your porcelainizing material. Blow off excess.**

[5]   **As this begins to set, add an additional coat or two, brushing with an extremely light "S" stroke, outward and away from surrounding areas. If you are using gold, the resulting effect will be that of pure gold.** *Do not glaze.* **Blow off excess gold dust.**

[6]   **Clean your brush.**

[7]   **Dip in acetone or lacquer thinner, and dryclean thoroughly.**

[8]   **Using a clean, dry brush, remove any flecks of the scattered gold, silver, or other metallic powder used.**

[9]   **Permit your work to set up. Reexamine for sharpness of color, tone, and perfection.**

[10]   **Perfect, as necessary, by repeating above steps.**

copper luster finish

Copper luster is made with high-gloss glaze and is very difficult to reproduce. You can buy gold powder from any art supply dealer. You will want a shade of gold called Roman Gold or Deep Rich Gold. Also, purchase some tubes of copper luster powder and some red iron oxide. This is a powder jewelers use for polishing. It can be bought in two-ounce containers. Blend colors into high-gloss New Gloss Glaze until you get a warm, rich amber. This color or shade may also be called dark, reddish-brown. Add copper until the mixture literally glows. Apply first coat and let it dry. Keep adding to colors until you have as exact a match as possible to your copper luster piece. Usually two or three layers will do the trick.

The final coating must be an overglaze of heavy high-gloss New Gloss Glaze. Feather it out over all surfaces so that all edges are blended into the surrounding areas.

bisque or wedgwood finishes

Usually articles made with these finishes are basically stoneware.

Wedgwood is a stoneware. The repairing of damages has been given in Chapter 2. The finishes are of a soft sheen.

To obtain a bisque finish you can soften any glaze by adding one or two pinches of plaster to thinner, and then add the solution to your glaze.

To obtain a Wedgwood finish, add a pinch or two of plaster or zinc oxide to thinner, and mix thoroughly until plaster or oxide is dissolved. Under window light, gradually add the color needed until you have an exact match. The addition of plaster or oxide will flatten the lacquer, color will not. But do not mix the paint or oil color and plaster any thicker than you have to, because Wedgwood has a translucency in its sheen that is very difficult to match.

chalkware finish

Articles of chalkware are repaired with plaster, so you will want to use plaster mixture in solvent with color added at a one-to-ten ratio to the lacquer, and then mix the two together to the shade desired. Chalkware may be grayish, white or buff. Naturally, any glaze or lacquer used will have to be completely flatted before application. The lacquer, when flatted, will give your mixture an adhesive quality and the final mix will, of course, conceal the mending.

appendix

---

useful
information

ready reference chart for systems and for terms and their meanings as used in this book

Mending: To cement (or glue) broken pieces together (handle broken in two pieces).

Repairing: To cement (or glue) broken out pieces back in place (cement handle in place, repair damages, fill in chips, etc., covers all damages).

Restore: To mold, model, or make a missing part, using System 1 (porcelainate), System 2 (for glass); System 3 (adhesive putty).

		CHINAWARE			CLEAR GLASS		POTTERY	
		hard paste true porcelain luminous hard transparent glaze	bone china hybrid type porcelain characteristic transparency	soft paste artificial porcelain	hard crystal flint lead	soft lime other	hard stoneware ironstone crockery	soft faience majolica porous
system 1	Mend	No	Yes	No	No	No	No	No
	Repair (Damages)	Yes	Yes	Yes	No	No	Yes	Yes
	Restore	Yes	Yes	Yes	No	No	Yes	Yes
system 2	Mend	Yes	Yes	Yes	Yes	Yes	Yes	No
	Repair	Yes	Yes	Yes	Yes	Yes	Yes	No
	Restore	Yes	Yes	Yes	Yes	Yes	Yes	No
system 3	Mend	No	No	No	No	No	No	Yes
	Repair (Damages)	Yes	Yes*	(Not Preferred)	No	No	Yes	Yes
	Restore	Yes	Yes*	(Not Preferred)	No	No	Yes	Yes

ready reference chart (continued)

| | CHINAWARE | | | OPAQUE GLASS | | POTTERY | |
	hard paste true porcelain luminous hard transparent glaze	bone china hybrid type porcelain characteristic transparency	soft paste artificial porcelain	hard crystal flint lead	soft lime other	hard stoneware ironstone crockery	soft faience majolica porous
system 4							
Mend	Yes	Yes	Yes	Colored	Colored	No	No
Repair	Yes	Yes	Yes	Colored	Colored	Yes	No
Restore	No	No	No	No	No	No	No
system 5 (glaze only)							
Mend	No	Yes	No	No	No	No	No
Repair	Yes	Yes	Yes	Yes	Yes	Yes	Yes
Restore	Yes	Yes	Yes	Yes	Yes	Yes	Yes

*To be used when making molds and restoring missing parts.

oriental export porcelain

TYPE	SYSTEMS TO USE		
hard paste	*mend*	*repair*	*restore*
China-Trade Porcelain *(Chinaware made and decorated in China according to Western design and decoration, chiefly in 18th century)*	2, 4	1, 2, and 4	1, 2, 4, and 5
Oriental Export Porcelain *(Includes all chinaware made in the Orient for export, chiefly to Europe, in 18th century)*	2, 4	1, 2, and 4	1, 2, 4, and 5
Oriental Lowestoft *(A misnomer sometimes used to describe Oriental Export chinaware. Has no connection with English Lowestoft)*	2, 4	1, 2, and 4	2, 3, 4, and 5
Imari *(Japanese porcelain, made from 17th century. Inferior in quality to China-Trade porcelain, but more elaborately decorated, sometimes using gold decoration)*	2, 4	1, 2, and 4	1, 2, 4, and 5
Kakiemon *(Japanese porcelain, made from 17th century, exported through port of Arita)*	2, 4	1, 2, and 4	1, 2, 4, and 5
Nankin (Nankeen) Canton Rose Medallion *(Types of Oriental Export Porcelain, made chiefly in early 19th century)*	2, 4	1, 2, and 4	1, 2, 3, 4, and 5

other types of oriental chinaware

TYPE	SYSTEMS TO USE		
hard paste	*mend*	*repair*	*restore*
Dynastic Chinaware *(Porcelain made in China from 8th and 9th centuries according to Chinese design and for Chinese use only. Dynastic decorations)*	*2, 4*	*1, 2, 4, and 5*	*1, 2, 3, 4, and 5*

continental european chinaware

TYPE	SYSTEMS TO USE		
hard paste	*mend*	*repair*	*restore*
Meissen *(Made at royal factory in Meissen from 1710 into early 19th century)*	*2, 4*	*1, 2, 4*	*1, 2, 4, 5*

Periods
Böttger   *1710–1719*
Höroldt-Kändler   *1720–1745*
Rococo   *1745–1774*
Marcolini   *1774–1814*

Dresden *(Term in use today to describe porcelain made in other factories in Dresden)*	*2, 4*	*1, 2, 4*	*1, 2, 4, 5*

continental european chinaware (continued)

TYPE	SYSTEMS TO USE		
hard paste	*mend*	*repair*	*restore*
Other German factories making hard paste chinaware in 18th century. Chinaware known today by name of city where manufactured:	2, 4	1, 2, 4	1, 2, 4, 5

	Founded about
Höchst	*1746*
Nymphenburg	*1747*
Berlin (Wegeley)	*1751*
Fürstenberg	*1753*
Frankenthal	*1755*
Ludwigsburg	*1756*

TYPE	mend	repair	restore
Austria	2, 4	1, 2, 4	1, 2, 4, 5
Vienna *1718*			

France

soft paste	2, 4	1, 2, 4	1, 2, 4, 5
Rouen *1763*			
St.-Cloud *1702–1765*			
Mennecy-Villeroy *1748*			
Vincennes *1745*			
Sevres *1745–1769*			

soft paste and hard paste			
Sevres *1769 to 1800* (clay deposits discovered at Limoges 1769)	2, 4	1, 2, 4	1, 2, 4, 5

hard paste			
Sevres after 1800	2, 4	1, 2, 4	1, 2, 4, 5

Denmark	2, 4	1, 2, 4	1, 2, 4, 5
Royal Copenhagen from 1773			

Italy

hard paste	2, 4	1, 2, 4	1, 2, 4, 5
Venice from about 1720			
soft paste			
Capo-di-Monte as early as 1743			

continental european chinaware (continued)

TYPE	SYSTEMS TO USE		
hard paste	*mend*	*repair*	*restore*
Spain	2, 4	1, 2, 4	1, 2, 4, 5
soft paste Buen Retiro from 1757			
English Chinaware *soft paste* Made in these famous factories up to the introduction of hard paste about 1770. Chelsea Derby Bow Bristol Worcester Spode Minton Lowestoft Caughley Coalport	2, 4	1, 2, 4	1, 2, 4, 5
hard paste "Cookworthy's Plymouth," first hard paste china made in England about 1770. Thereafter, most of the factories made some hard paste chinaware.	2, 4	1, 2, 4	1, 2, 4, 5
Bone china: This type of china- ware was developed between 1790– 1810. Thereafter, most English factories began using this type, and it is the principal type of English china made today. Familiar names: Spode, Worcester Royal Porcelain, Royal Crown Derby.	2, 4	1, 2, 4	1, 2, 4, 5

american chinaware

MANUFACTURER	SYSTEMS TO USE		
	mend	*repair*	*restore*
Pickard Inc. (level with Lenox)	*2, 4*	*1, 2, 4*	*1, 2, 4, 5*
Buffalo China Co. (vitreous)	*2, 4*	*1, 2, 4*	*1, 2, 4, 5*
American Haviland & Company	*2, 4*	*1, 2, 4*	*1, 2, 4, 5*
Iroquois China—Syracuse China Co.	*2, 4*	*1, 2, 4*	*1, 2, 4, 5*
Hyalyn Porcelain Ware	*2, 4*	*1, 2, 4*	*1, 2, 4, 5*
Crooksville China Co.	*2, 4*	*1, 2, 4*	*1, 2, 4, 5*
Hall China Co.	*2, 4*	*1, 2, 4*	*1, 2, 4, 5*
Laughlin-Homer Co.	*2, 4*	*1, 2, 4*	*1, 2, 4, 5*
Salem China Co.	*2, 4*	*1, 2, 4*	*1, 2, 4, 5*
French Saxon Co.	*2, 4*	*1, 2, 4*	*1, 2, 4, 5*
Royal China Co.	*2, 4*	*1, 2, 4*	*1, 2, 4, 5*
Chenango Ceramics	*2, 4*	*1, 2, 4*	*1, 2, 4, 5*
Cordey	*2, 4*	*1, 2, 4*	*1, 2, 4, 5*
Atlas Crystal and Commemorative Porcelain Co.	*2, 4*	*1, 2, 4*	*1, 2, 4, 5*
Sun Prairie Porcelains	*2, 4*	*1, 2, 4*	*1, 2, 4, 5*
Lenox	*2, 4*	*1, 2, 4*	*1, 2, 4, 5*

oriental glass

clear	colored	opaque	mend	repair	restore
	TYPE			SYSTEMS TO USE	
Fei-ts-ui-Peking			2	2	2, 5
	Peking		2	2, 5	2, 5
		Peking	2	1, 2, 5	1, 2, 4, 5
Shin-Mao			2	2	2, 5
	Shin-Mao		2	2	2, 5
		Shin-Mao	2	1, 2, 5	1, 2, 4, 5
Ku-Yueh Husan			2	2	2, 5
	Ku-Yueh Husan		2	2	2, 5
		Ku-Yueh Husan	2	1, 2, 5	1, 2, 4, 5
Fu-Lions			2		
	Fu-Lions			2, 5	
		Fu-Lions		2, 5	1, 2, 4, 5
Yeh-Chung San			2		
	Yeh-Chung San			2, 5	
		Yeh-Chung San			1, 2, 4, 5
Shou			2		
	Shou			2, 5	
		Shou			1, 2, 4, 5
Chien Lung			2		
	Chien Lung			2, 5	
		Chien Lung			1, 2, 4, 5
Hu Peking Po-Shan			2	2, 5	2, 5

continental european glass

clear	colored	opaque	mend	repair	restore
	TYPE			SYSTEMS TO USE	
Baccarat			2	2	2, 5
	Baccarat		2	1, 2	1, 2, 5
	Fabergé		2	1, 2	1, 2, 5
		Fabergé	2	1, 2	1, 2, 4, 5
Gallé			2	1, 2	1, 2, 5
	Gallé		2	1, 2	1, 2, 5
		Gallé	2	1, 2	1, 2, 4, 5
	Opal		2	1, 2	1, 2, 4, 5
		Opaline	2	1, 2	1, 2, 4, 5
	Iridescent		2	1, 2	1, 2, 5
		Iridescent	2	1, 2	1, 2, 4, 5
Alexandrite			2		
	Alexandrite			2, 5	
Bohemian			2		
	Bohemian			2, 5	
		Bohemian			1, 2, 4, 5
	Dalton Nancy		2	2, 5	1, 2, 4, 5
	French Cameo		2	2, 5	
	DeBez		2	2, 5	
	(cased)		2	2, 5	
		Lalique			1, 2, 4, 5
		Loetz			1, 2, 4, 5
Depression Glass	Montjoye				
	(enameled)				1, 2, 4, 5

anglo-irish glass

| TYPE | | | SYSTEMS TO USE | | |
clear	colored	opaque	mend	repair	restore
	Beilby		2	2	2, 5
Bristol			2	2	2, 5
	Bristol		2	2	2, 5
		Bristol	2	2	1, 2, 4, 5
	Cameo		2	2	1, 2, 5
		Cameo Cut	2	2	1, 2, 4, 5
Cased			2	2	1, 2
	Cased		2	2	1, 2, 5
		Cased	2	2	1, 2, 4, 5
Nailsea			2	2	1, 2, 5
	Nailsea		2	2	1, 2, 5
		Nailsea	2	2	1, 2, 4, 5
	Stourbridge		2	2	2, 5
		Stourbridge	2	2	1, 2, 4, 5
Ravenscraft			2	2	1, 2, 5
		Webb (cased)	2	2	1, 2, 4, 5
		Stevens & Williams	2	2	1, 2, 4, 5
		Nacara	2	2	1, 2, 4, 5

american glass

clear	colored	opaque	mend	repair	restore
	Amberina (New England)		2	2	1, 2, 4, 5
		Agata	2	2	1, 2, 4, 5
		Burmese (Washington)	2	2	1, 2, 4, 5
		Cluthra	2	2	1, 2, 4, 5
	Amethyst		2	2	1, 2, 4, 5
Blown Glass			2	1, 2	1, 2, 5
	Blown Glass		2	1, 2	1, 2, 5
Hob Nail			2	1, 2	1, 2, 5
	Hob Nail		2	1, 2	1, 2, 5
	Iridescent		2	1, 2	1, 2, 5
Imperial			2	2, 5	2, 5
	Imperial		2	2	
		Imperial	2	1, 2	1, 2, 4, 5
	Kew Blas		2	2	
		Kew Blas	2	1, 2	1, 2, 4, 5
Beam			2	2, 5	2, 5
	Beam		2	1, 2	1, 2, 5
		Cambridge	2	1, 2	1, 2, 4, 5
	Carnival		2	2	2
		Coralene	2	2	1, 2, 4, 5
Crackle			2	2, 5	2, 5
	Crackle		2	2	
	Milk Glass		2	1, 2	1, 2
		Milk Glass	2	1, 2	1, 2, 4, 5
	Crown Milano		2	1, 2	1, 2, 5
		Crown Milano	2	1, 2	1, 2, 4, 5
		Custard Glass	2	1, 2	1, 2, 4, 5
Cut Glass					
(Hawks)			2	2	2, 5
(Libby)			2	2	2, 5
(Woodall)			2	2	2, 5
(Clarke)			2	2	2, 5
(Hoars)			2	2	2, 5
(St. Claire)			2	2	2, 5
Depression Glass			2	2, 5	2, 5
	Depression Glass		2	2	2, 5

american glass (continued)

TYPE			SYSTEMS TO USE		
clear	*colored*	*opaque*	*mend*	*repair*	*restore*
	Finley or Onyx (cased)		2	2	2, 5
Fostoria (etched)			2	2, 5	2, 5
	Fostoria (etched)		2	2	2, 5
	Fry		2	2	2, 5
		Fry	2	1, 2	1, 2, 5
Heisey			2	2, 5	2, 5
	Heisey		2	2	2, 5
	Holly Amber		2	2, 5	2, 5
		Holly Amber	2	1, 2	1, 2, 4, 5
		Lotus Ware	2	1, 2	1, 2, 4, 5
Mary Gregory			2	2, 5	2, 5
	Mary Gregory (enameled)		2	2	1, 2, 4, 5
Moser			2	2, 5	2, 5
	Moser		2	2, 5	2, 5
		Mother-of-Pearl	2	1, 2, 5	1, 2, 4, 5
		Mt. Washington	2	1, 2, 5	1, 2, 4, 5
	Mt. Washington		2	1, 2, 5	1, 2, 4, 5
Mt. Washington		Mt. Washington	2	2, 5	1, 2, 4, 5
		Nash (cased)	2	1, 2, 5	1, 2, 4, 5
Nash			2	2, 5	2, 5
	Nash		2	2, 5	2, 5
Northwood			2	2, 5	2, 5
	Northwood		2	2, 5	2, 5
	Opalescent		2	1, 2, 5	1, 2, 5
		Opaline Peach Blow	2	1, 2, 5	1, 2, 4, 5
Phoenix (etched)			2	2	2, 5
Pomona			2	2	2, 5
	Pomona		2	2	2, 5
Pressed Glass (camphor)			2	2, 5	2, 5
	Pressed Glass (camphor)		2	2	2, 5

american glass (continued)

	TYPE		SYSTEMS TO USE		
clear	colored	opaque	mend	repair	restore
		Pressed Glass (camphor)	2	2	2, 5
Pittsburgh			2	2	2, 5
	Pittsburgh		2	2	2, 5
		Pittsburgh	2	1, 2	1, 2, 4, 5
		Royal Flemish	2	1, 2	1, 2, 4, 5
Sandwich Glass			2	2, 5	1, 2, 5
	Sandwich		2	2, 5	1, 2, 5
		Sandwich	2	2, 5	1, 2, 4, 5
		Satin	2	2, 5	1, 2, 4, 5
Schneider (crystal)			2	2	2, 5
Silver Deposit			2	2	1, 2, 4, 5
	Silver Deposit		2	2	1, 2, 4, 5
		Stag	2	2	1, 2, 4, 5
		Spangled Glass	2	2	1, 2, 4, 5
		Spatter Glass	2	2	1, 2, 4, 5
		Star Holly	2	2	1, 2, 4, 5
Steuben			2	2, 5	1, 2, 5
	Steuben		2	2	
		Steuben	2	2, 5	1, 2, 4, 5
Tiffany			2	2, 5	1, 2, 5
	Tiffany		2	2, 5	2, 5
		Tiffany	2	2, 5	2, 5
	Vasa Murrhina		2	2, 5	2, 5
		Vasa Murrhina	2	1, 2, 5	1, 2, 4, 5
	Vasart		2	2, 5	2, 5
		Vasart	2	1, 2, 5	1, 2, 4, 5
Verlys (crystal)			2	2, 5	2, 5
Verre di Soir			2	2	2, 5
	Verre di Soir		2	2	2, 5
		Verre di Soir	2	2	1, 2, 4, 5

oriental pottery

TYPE		SYSTEMS TO USE		
hard paste	soft paste	mend	repair	restore
Japan				
Dai Nippon		1	1, 5	1, 4, 5
	Dai Nippon	1	1, 5	1, 4, 5
Kutani		1	1, 5	1, 4, 5
	Yayoi	3	3, 5	3, 4, 5
	Hawiwa	3	3, 5	3, 4, 5

english pottery

TYPE	SYSTEMS TO USE		
hard paste	mend	repair	restore
Burslem			
(Ironstone)	1, 2	1, 2, 5	1, 2, 4, 5
Caughley Fenton			
(Mason)	1, 2	1, 2, 5	1, 2, 4, 5
Whieldon	1, 2	1, 2, 5	1, 2, 4, 5
Fulham	1, 2	1, 2, 5	1, 2, 4, 5
Lambeth	1, 2	1, 2, 5	1, 2, 4, 5
Doulton	1, 2	1, 2, 5	1, 2, 4, 5
Herculaneum	1, 2	1, 2, 5	1, 2, 4, 5
Cauldon	1, 2	1, 2, 5	1, 2, 4, 5
Imperial Stone	1, 2	1, 2, 5	1, 2, 4, 5
Staffordshire	1, 2	1, 2, 5	1, 2, 4, 5
Minton	1, 2	1, 2, 5	1, 2, 4, 5
Spode	1, 2	1, 2, 5	1, 2, 4, 5
Swansea	1, 2	1, 2, 5	1, 2, 4, 5
Rockingham	1, 2	1, 2, 5	1, 2, 4, 5
Wedgwood	1, 2	1, 2, 5	1, 2, 4, 5
Etruria	1, 2	1, 2, 5	1, 2, 4, 5
Worcester	1, 2	1, 2, 5	1, 2, 4, 5

continental european pottery

TYPE		SYSTEMS TO USE		
hard paste	*soft paste*	*mend*	*repair*	*restore*
	Belgium			
	Liege	2	*2, 5*	*1, 2, 4, 5*
	Copenhagen	2	*2, 4, 5*	*1, 2, 4, 5*
	Naestved Danish			
	China Works	2	*2, 4, 5*	*1, 2, 4, 5*
	France			
	Aprey	2	*1 or 3, 4, 5*	*1 or 3 2, 4, 5*
	Apt	2	*1 or 3, 4, 5*	*1 or 3 2, 4, 5*
	Blois	2	*1 or 3, 4, 5*	*1 or 3 2, 4, 5*
	Lille	2	*1 or 3, 4, 5*	*1 or 3 2, 4, 5*
	Sarreguemines	2	*1 or 3, 4, 5*	*1, 2, 4, 5*
Sceaux		2	*1, 2, 4, 5*	*1, 2, 4, 5*
Sèvres Biscuit		2		*1, 2, 4, 5*
	Germany			
	Bernburg	2	*2, 5*	*2, 3, 4, 5*
	Damm	2	*2, 5*	*2, 3, 4, 5*
	Diemstein	2	*2, 5*	*2, 3, 4, 5*
Mettlach	*Mettlach*	2	*2, 5*	*2, 3, 4, 5*
	Minden	2	*2, 5*	*2, 3, 4, 5*
Persia	Persia	2	*2, 5*	*2, 3, 4, 5*
Turkey	Turkey	2	*2, 5*	*2, 3, 4, 5*
Syria	Syria	2	*2, 5*	*2, 3, 4, 5*
	Poland			
	Stawsk	2	*1, 2, 5*	*1, 2, 4, 5*
	Spain			
	Faience			
	Majolica	2	*2, 3, 5*	
	Holland			
	Delft	2	*1, 2, 5*	*1, 2, 4, 5*
	Italy			
Capo di Monte	*Semi Porcelain*	2	*1, 2, 5*	*1, 2, 4, 5*
	Faenza	2	*2, 3, 5*	*2, 3, 5*
	Majolica	2	*2, 3, 5*	*2, 3, 5*
Forli		2	*1, 2, 5*	*1, 2, 4, 5*

continental european pottery (continued)

TYPE		SYSTEMS TO USE		
hard paste	soft paste	mend	repair	restore
Italy (*continued*)				
Genoa		2	1, 2, 5	1, 2, 4, 5
Norway				
	Luxembourg	2	2, 3, 5	2, 3, 5
Sweden				
Fayence		2	1, 2, 5	1, 2, 4, 5
Russia				
	St. Petersburg	2	2, 3, 5	1, 2, 4, 5
Moscow		2	1, 2, 5	1, 2, 4, 5
Kiev		2	1, 2, 5	1, 2, 4, 5

american pottery

TYPE		SYSTEMS TO USE		
hard paste	soft paste	mend	repair	restore
East Liverpool				
Ironstone		1, 2	1, 2, 5	1, 2, 4, 5
Greenpoint				
	Faience	3, 5	3, 5	3, 5
Birmington, Vt.				
Fenton	Earthenware	2, 3	1, 3, 5	3, 4, 5
Glasgow, N.J.				
	Potterywares	2, 3	3, 5	3, 5
Globe				
Earthenwares		2, 3	1, 3, 5	2, 3, 4, 5
Ironstones		2, 3	1, 3, 5	2, 3, 4, 5
Grueby				
	Faience	3	3, 5	3, 4, 5

american pottery (continued)

TYPE		SYSTEMS TO USE		
hard paste	*soft paste*	*mend*	*repair*	*restore*
Knowles, Taylor				
Stoneware		*2, 3*	*1, 3*	*2, 3, 4, 5*
Ironstone		*3*	*5*	*2, 3, 4, 5*
	Semi Porcelain	*2, 3*	*1, 3*	*2, 3, 4, 5*
John Maddock				
Ironstone		*2, 3*	*1, 3*	*2, 3, 4, 5*
Akron				
Ironstone		*2*	*2, 4, 5*	*2, 3, 4, 5*
Jersey City				
American		*2*	*2, 4, 5*	*2, 3, 4, 5*
Pottery		*2*	*2, 4, 5*	*2, 3, 4, 5*
Ironstone		*2*	*2, 4, 5*	*2, 3, 4, 5*
Trenton, N.J.				
Anchor		*2*	*2, 4, 5*	*2, 3, 4, 5*
Earthenware		*2*	*2, 4, 5*	*2, 3, 4, 5*
Buffalo Pottery				
Ironstone		*2*	*2, 4, 5*	*2, 3, 4, 5*
Chesapeake				
(Severn)		*2*	*2, 4, 5*	*2, 3, 4, 5*
Earthenwares		*2*	*2, 4, 5*	*2, 3, 4, 5*
Phoenixville				
	Slipwares	*2*	*3*	*3, 5*
Earthenwares		*2*	*2, 3, 5*	*3, 5*
Crescent				
Ironstone		*1, 2*	*1, 2, 5*	*1, 2, 4, 5*
	Semi-Porcelain	*1, 2*	*1, 2, 5*	*1, 2, 4, 5*
Crown Pottery				
Semi Vitreous		*3*	*5*	*3, 5*
	Faience	*2*	*3, 5*	*3, 4, 5*
Matt Morgan				
Art Pottery				
	Art Pottery	*3*	*3*	*3, 5*
New England Pottery				
	Art Pottery	*3*	*3*	*3, 5*
Stoneware		*2, 3*	*2, 3, 5*	*2, 3, 4, 5*
Ott & Brewer				
"Belleek"		*1, 2*	*1, 2, 5*	*1, 2, 4, 5*

american pottery (continued)

TYPE		SYSTEMS TO USE		
hard paste	soft paste	mend	repair	restore
Onondaga Pottery				
Syracuse		*1, 2*	*1, 2, 5*	*1, 2, 4, 5*
Ironstone		*1, 2*	*1, 2, 5*	*1, 2, 4, 5*
Rookwood				
Ironstone		*1, 2*	*1, 2, 5*	*1, 2, 4, 5*
	Faience	*3*	*3, 5*	*1, 2, 4, 5*
Earthenwares		*1, 2*	*1, 2, 5*	*1, 2, 4, 5*
	Art Wares	*3*	*3, 5*	*3, 5*
Sebring				
Stoneware		*1, 2*	*1, 2, 5*	*1, 2, 4, 5*
Trenton				
	Tiles	*1, 2*	*1, 2, 5*	*1, 2, 4, 5*
Weller				
	Earthenwares	*3*	*3, 5*	*3, 5*
Wheeling				
	Earthenwares	*3*	*3, 5*	*3, 5*

index